CHRISTIAN HEROES: THEN & NOW

DAVID LIVINGSTONE

Africa's Trailblazer

D0950794

CHRISTIAN HEROES: THEN & NOW

DAVID LIVINGSTONE

Africa's Trailblazer

JANET & GEOFF BENGE

YWAM
PUBLISHING

P.O. BOX 55787   SEATTLE, WA 98155

YWAM Publishing is the publishing ministry of Youth With A Mission. Youth With A Mission (YWAM) is an international missionary organization of Christians from many denominations dedicated to presenting Jesus Christ to this generation. To this end, YWAM has focused its efforts in three main areas: (1) training and equipping believers for their part in fulfilling the Great Commission (Matthew 28:19), (2) personal evangelism, and (3) mercy ministry (medical and relief work).

For a free catalog of books and materials, contact:

YWAM Publishing
P.O. Box 55787, Seattle, WA 98155
(425) 771-1153 or (800) 922-2143
www.ywampublishing.com

David Livingstone: Africa's Trailblazer

10 09 08 07 06 05 04 03   10 9 8 7 6 5 4 3

Published by Youth With A Mission Publishing
P.O. Box 55787
Seattle, WA 98155

ISBN 1-57658-153-5

Printed in the United States of America.

CHRISTIAN HEROES: THEN & NOW
Biographies

Gladys Aylward
Rowland Bingham
Corrie ten Boom
William Booth
William Carey
Amy Carmichael
Loren Cunningham
Jim Elliot
Jonathan Goforth
Betty Greene
Wilfred Grenfell
Adoniram Judson
Eric Liddell
David Livingstone
Lottie Moon
George Müller
Nate Saint
Ida Scudder
Mary Slessor
Hudson Taylor
Cameron Townsend
Lillian Trasher
John Williams

*Unit study curriculum guides
are available for these biographies.*

Available at your local Christian bookstore or
YWAM Publishing
1 (800) 922-2143

Africa

Southern Africa During the Time of David Livingstone

N

Lualaba River

Nyangwe

Lake Victoria

Ujiji

Zanzibar

Lake Tanganika

Loanda

Pungo Andongo

Lake Bangwelo

Mikindani

Rovuma River

Lake Nyasa

Lake Shirwa

Zambezi River

Tete

Magomero

Shire River

Sesheke

Linyanti

Victoria Falls

Quilimane

Lake Ngami

Zouga River

Chonuane

Kolobeng

Mabotsa

Indian Ocean

Atlantic Ocean

Kuruman

Cape Town

Port Elizabeth

0	200	400 miles
0	½	1 inch
	Scale	

Contents

Chapter 1

Still Alive

Something moved in the undergrowth. David Livingstone stopped in his tracks. Suddenly he saw the flick of a tail, a tan-colored tail with a tuft at the end. As he looked closer he could make out the shape of a lion hidden among the bushes. Not a small lion, but one that must have weighed at least four hundred pounds, and now it was no more than ten feet away.

Without taking his eyes off the huge animal for one second, David reached over his shoulder for his rifle. He put the stock of the gun to his shoulder and lined up the sights with the lion's eyes. Smoothly he squeezed the trigger. Boom! The mouth of the rifle exploded in a flash of burning gunpowder. The lead bullet found its mark, slamming into the lion's neck.

11

But instead of falling over dead, the lion stood roaring in agony. David watched in amazement as it crouched back on its haunches and then leapt forward.

The rifle flew from David Livingstone's hand. Pain raced through David's body as the lion's jaws clamped down hard on his left arm, each of the lion's razor-sharp teeth cutting into his flesh. Before David knew what was happening, the beast had lifted him into the air and was shaking him like a cat shaking a mouse. Then it dropped him and pounced again, tightening its vicelike grip on his arm. David felt the lion's hot breath against his body and its saliva seeping through his torn jacket. The animal rested its paw on David's head, and David could feel the point of each claw poised to rip his skull open. Through the searing pain in his body, David could feel his heart thumping wildly in his chest. He was dimly aware of shouting in the background, but his world had narrowed to just him and the lion, and the lion was winning. Again the lion raised David effortlessly into the air and shook him. This time, David felt his skin ripping and bones breaking.

Boom! Another gunshot rang out, and the lion dropped David Livingstone like a sack of corn. David lay on the ground stunned and in numbing pain for a second and then rolled over. "God help us," he cried when he saw the lion crouching yet again. Would nothing kill it? The lion lunged at David's helper, Mebalwe. The African fell to the ground as the lion locked its huge mouth around Mebalwe's thigh.

The men from the village, who had been standing stunned and motionless as the attack took place around them, suddenly sprang into action. Five, ten, fifteen spears were hurled at the lion. The lion made a final leap at yet another man, but the combined effect of the gunshots and the spears finally took their toll, and the lion fell over dead. That was the last thing David Livingstone remembered before he slipped into unconsciousness.

When David came around fifteen minutes later, he found himself lying on the veranda of the mission house at Mabotsa. Fellow missionary Roger Edwards was anxiously bending over him, dabbing his wound gingerly with a damp cloth.

Dazed, David tried to sit up. Searing pain shot up his left arm and through his body. He remembered the cracking of bone and the lion's teeth buried deep in his arm. Then all the other details of the attack came flooding back to him. Shocked, he realized he'd survived. But what about Mebalwe? Had he survived? David grasped Roger Edwards's arm with his right hand and asked about his helper.

"Yes, he's alive," Edwards assured him. "He has deep wounds on his leg from the teeth, but I don't think anything is broken."

Relieved, David slumped back down onto his back. At least no one had died trying to save him. And although most people attacked by lions in the wild were killed, somehow he had survived. It was

all such a long way from Scotland, where the wildest
animals he had encountered were the sheep that
grazed on the hillside around the town of Blantyre
where he had grown up. If the people back there
could see him now....

Chapter 2

Different from Everyone Else

Twelve-year-old David Livingstone held his breath as he waited for his father to answer.

"So, you want to go out into the hills?" asked Mr. Livingstone, stroking his beard. "Let me see now. What was your memory verse from Sunday school this morning, David?"

"Matthew chapter four, verse four. 'It is written, man shall not live by bread alone, but by every word that proceeds out of the mouth of God,'" replied David confidently.

"Very good, son," said his father, patting David's light brown hair. Then turning to Grandpa Livingstone, who was propped in a straight-backed, wooden chair in the corner of the dimly lit room, he added, "Of course, that's an easy verse for David.

15

He could recite the whole of Psalm 119 when he was nine. He won a new Bible for his effort."

David felt himself blushing. His father never complimented him directly or told him he was proud of his son, but he did like to tell other people about David's accomplishments.

"Can we go, Dad? Please…?" begged Charles, David's younger brother.

"A little fresh air can't hurt the boys on the Lord's day," interjected Grandpa Livingstone, who lived in a room two floors below. "After all, the lads are cooped up from dawn to dusk every day. A laddie needs to get out in the open and smell the heather. When I was a lad, I lived my whole life in the open air. I can still shut my eyes and see the black rocks of the Isle of Ulva and smell the peat fires we lit to keep us warm on those nights when we had the sheep up in the high pastures to graze."

David looked urgently at his father. If his grandfather got started on stories from his childhood in the Scottish highlands, there was no telling how long David and his two brothers would be stuck inside.

Thankfully, David's father seemed to understand the predicament. "I'll put on a pot of the new tea that just arrived from China, and we'll sit and talk a spell while the boys run out to play," he said. Then turning to John, David's older brother by two years, he added, "Be back before dark, and mind your manners if you meet anyone along the way."

"We will, Father," the three boys chorused as they rushed out the door.

As David ran along the cobblestone road that led from the town of Blantyre into the surrounding countryside, he could feel the book bumping against the side of his leg. The reminder of what lay ahead made him run faster.

Finally, completely out of breath, the three brothers flopped down in their favorite spot, a lush, grassy plateau located on the side of a hill about three hundred feet above the town. Below, the boys could see Blantyre and its rows of crumbling brick apartment houses. They could also see the Clyde River as it snaked its way through the town, and since it was such a clear day, the city of Glasgow was visible eight miles off in the distance.

"Look, I can see Shuttle Row. Which one is our room?" asked Charles, plonking himself down beside David.

"Our room is on the other side of the mill," replied David, looking at the gloomy row of brick tenements that flanked the huge cotton mill.

The three boys sat side by side for a few minutes taking in the view. It always fascinated David to be up high looking down at the world.

"Let's run some more," said Charles, interrupting David's thoughts.

"Not right now," replied David, untying the string he had wound around the bottom of his trouser leg and carefully extracting the book from inside his pants.

Charles gasped. "You're not supposed to read that," he said. "Dad told you not to."

"There's no harm in it, and if you know what's good for you, you'll keep your mouth shut," David replied.

"Come on, Charles, let's leave David to his book. I'll give you a head start, and then I'll chase you," said John.

The two boys ran off farther up the hill while David rolled onto his belly in the soft grass and opened *Culpepper's Herbal*. The book contained row after row of drawings of plants. The stalk, leaves, flower, and seed of each plant were rendered in meticulous detail, and underneath each drawing was the plant's scientific name. David studied the pictures closely and was soon lost in the pages of the book. He recognized many of the plants from his walks in the hills. One or two of them even grew around the tenement building where his family rented a single-room apartment, but many of the plants were foreign to him. He wished he could see them and pick their leaves and press them for his collection, although he knew that would not be likely. Indeed, it was unlikely he'd ever go farther afield than a mile or two from the place where he had been born and raised. Few people ever did. In fact, David had never even been to Glasgow. Once when David asked to be taken there for a visit, his father had simply asked why he would want to go to a smoky, miserable city like that. His father didn't seem to share David's urge to see things for the sake of seeing them. But then, neither could his father understand why reading a botany book was so important. So important to David that he was willing to risk being punished for disobeying his father's express instruction not to read such a book.

David found it hard to accept that his father did not want him to learn anything about science. Like many people in the early nineteenth century, his father thought science and religion were incompatible. Mr. Livingstone argued that it went against the laws of God to be asking why things were the way they were or seeking to discover the inner workings of plants or animals. He told David many times that people should be happy with things the way the good Lord made them and not concern themselves with the hows and whys.

But David was not happy accepting things the way they were, and that made him different from everyone else he knew. At the Monteith & Co. cotton mill, where he and his brother John worked fourteen hours a day six days a week, he was an oddity whom the other children made fun of. His job was commonplace enough. David was a piecer, and there were three piecers for every weaver. A piecer was a young person, boy or girl, who ran or crawled between the great clanking looms watching for threads that had broken. The piecer's job was to quickly tie the broken threads together before they made a run in the fabric. If the piecer was not quick enough at this, the fabric would have a blemish in it. When this happened, the weaver would swat the piecer across the back with a leather strap. It was grim work, and the noise of the looms, the hissing of steam, and the grinding of machines made talking impossible. So David passed the time with a book. He would prop it open on a cotton bale, and whenever he had a few seconds to spare, he would glance at it and read a sentence. This gave him something to think about while he worked and until he could read another sentence.

The other piecers would throw empty cotton reels at David's book, laughing and slapping each other on the back when they hit the cover and sent the book flying. When David was younger, he had yelled insults at them. Now that he was twelve, he just smiled and kept working.

Thankfully, David's mother's father, Grandpa Hunter, lived nearby. David had inherited his love of reading from him, and although he was not a rich man, Grandpa Hunter owned a large collection of books. He lent books to David and did not tell Mr. Livingstone when David borrowed a science book to read. David read other books, too. In fact he was just beginning to learn to read Latin.

About the time that David's Grandpa Livingstone had migrated from the countryside to Blantyre, the British government had passed a law making it compulsory for factories and mills to offer schooling to any child under twelve years of age whom they employed. The owners of the mill where David and his brother John worked obeyed the law. However, the law didn't state at what time the classes should be offered, so the classes were held from eight until ten each night, after the children had worked their fourteen-hour shift. Of course, most of the children were far too tired to take advantage of the classes. As a result, only about one in ten of them ever learned to read.

David Livingstone, who had been taught to read by his father when he was only six, was more determined than the average student. He forced himself to stay awake, not only for the classes but also to read his schoolbooks late into the night. More often than not, his mother would have to take the books from him and blow out his candle. Even then, David would lie awake for hours thinking about what he'd read, trying to recall it word for word.

"David. David. Come here. I've got something to show you," Charles's voice rang out through the hills.

David looked up from his botany book and frowned. The sun was far to the west—an hour or more must have passed since he had started reading. David scrambled to his feet. "Coming," he yelled, tucking the book under his arm.

"Look what I found," Charles proudly yelled as David came closer, his chubby little finger pointing at the ground.

David followed his brother's finger. Charles was pointing to a tiny skeleton about the size of a mouse.

"What is it?" Charles asked.

"I don't know yet," replied David, bending down for a closer look. "Let's see. Is it a bird or an animal?" he asked, turning to his little brother.

Charles shrugged. "How can we tell?" he inquired.

"Well," said David, "let's think of something a bird has that say a mouse doesn't. Then we'll look and see if those bones are there."

"Wings," Charles shot back proudly. "Mice don't have wings!"

"That's a good start," replied David. "Now let's see if we can see any wing bones."

The three boys examined the skeleton and came to the conclusion that indeed it did have wing bones and so must be the skeleton of a small bird, though David could not tell exactly what kind of bird.

"I'm going to find another skeleton," yelled Charles as he raced off.

David smiled. He dared not tell Charles that what they'd just done was "science." There was so much science to be done in the world, and it seemed a great pity to David that it was so unchristian to think about it and pursue it.

The afternoon sped by, and before long, the brothers were racing down the hill towards Shuttle Row. Their father had a strict rule on Sunday that anyone who came home after sundown had to spend the night sleeping outside on the doorstep. Since all three boys had endured this hardship more than once, they were eager to be on time. When they got back, Grandpa Livingstone was still telling stories and drinking tea.

"They're home. The boys are home, Ma," squealed seven-year-old Janet, in obvious delight that her brothers were back.

David patted Janet on the head and tickled baby Agnes.

"Take off your coats, and I'll pour you a cup of tea," said Mrs. Livingstone, reaching for the huge copper teapot that hung over the hearth. She poured three cups of the hot brew and stirred two spoonfuls of sugar into each one. She handed a cup to each of her three sons.

David took a deep whiff of the tea. "Is this the new blend?" he asked his father.

"Yes," Mr. Livingstone replied. "I think I like it."

David took a sip. "Me too," he said.

Mr. Livingstone smiled. "I have three sacks of it, so I hope it sells well."

David nodded. He understood how important it was for his father to choose popular blends of tea. Mr. Livingstone was a tea peddler. He bought sacks of tea from a wagon that came through from Glasgow, repackaged them into small bags, and walked the length and breadth of Lanarkshire selling them door to door. Although this did not produce much money for his growing family, it did allow him to do the one thing he loved most of all. Wherever he went, Mr. Livingstone talked about God, prayed for people, and gave away hundreds of Christian tracts. When he got home each night, he would tell the children all about the adventures of his day. To children who spent fourteen hours a day in a hot, stuffy mill, they were the most exciting stories they had ever heard.

The following morning, David rose with the rest of the family at five o'clock. (The single room they all shared made it impossible for anyone to sleep late.) It was the start of another long week at the mill. After eating their bowls of porridge, David and John walked to the mill together, joining the throng of other youngsters headed there. As they walked, David looked at the other children. They all had so much in common. They were all poor and had been sent to work at a young age to help their parents pay the rent on the single-room apartments they lived in. David wondered whether this was the life he would always lead. Would he grow up and marry one of the girls from the mill? Would his children walk the same street to work in the same mill? David could see his life stretched out in front of him like the continuous reams of cotton he watched over each day. It was a life of working six days a week, attending church on Sunday, and snatching time to read whenever he could.

Never in his wildest imagination could David Livingstone have dreamed how different his life was destined to be.

Chapter 3

Rotten Row

Science or religion? The choice had haunted David Livingstone for eight years now. David wanted to become a Christian, but so many wonderful scientific discoveries were taking place in the world that it was hard for him to think of turning his back on them to give his life to God.

David constantly puzzled over the dilemma before him, until 1832, when a book came to his rescue. *Philosophy of a Future State* by Dr. Dick was loaned to David by the Reverend Moir, pastor of the Congregational Church the Livingstone family attended. Although the title of the book did not sound exciting, the book's contents grabbed David's attention from the start. Dr. Dick was a thoroughly Christian man, and in the book he argued that God was a scientific designer and that the diligent study of biology, botany, chemistry, and astronomy would draw the student closer to God. According to Dr. Dick, who was himself a famous Scottish astronomer, a person could pursue both God and science. The two could go together! David was stunned. This was exactly what he had thought, but he'd never found any evidence that others agreed with him. Now he was free to become a Christian without having to reject science and a knowledge of the natural world around him.

After praying and asking God to guide his life, David was still a little unsure how to go about telling his father that he wanted to pursue science and that it wasn't an evil thing to know about the insides of the body or the reason why the stars crossed the night sky.

Thankfully, something happened that changed David's father's mind. At church, the Reverend Moir read a long letter, entitled *To the Churches of Britain and America on Behalf of China,* to the congregation from a Dr. Charles Gutzlaff. In the letter Dr. Gutzlaff told of the tremendous need for missionaries in China and recommended medical training as the best kind of training for a missionary. As a doctor, a missionary could speak to the people about God while healing them physically. As David sat next to his father listening to the letter being read aloud, his heart raced. Here was a missionary suggesting that a man get medical training, *scientific* training, before going to the mission field! Here, at last, was a reason why a Christian should learn about science.

As the family walked the three miles home from church that morning, David and his father fell into step together. "So what did you think of Dr. Gutzlaff's letter?" David asked nervously, afraid his father would disagree wholeheartedly with it.

"Fascinating, fascinating," replied Mr. Livingstone. "Perhaps I've been a little harsh in regard to learning about science. If science can open a Chinese man's heart to God, it must have some merit after all."

David could hardly believe what he was hearing. Did his father mean it? He had to know. "So you wouldn't mind if I borrowed a few books about medicine to read?" he asked, almost afraid of the answer.

His father walked in silence for several minutes. "No, lad," he finally said, and then added, "but I don't know what good it will do you working in the mill and all."

Mixed emotions surged through David. On the one hand, his father was giving him permission to pursue science. On the other hand, it was true—he worked at the mill for fourteen hours a day. He was nineteen years old, he still lived at home, and nearly every penny he earned went towards paying the rent for the family apartment and funding the three younger children's education. David only wished he could have had the same chance at education as his younger siblings, but it was too late now. Still, somehow, he assured himself, he was going to become a medical missionary.

When he told his grandfather of his plans, Grandpa Livingstone tried to sound enthusiastic. Deep down, though, David knew he was worried about any of his grandchildren leaving Blantyre. Grandpa Livingstone had had five sons. Three of them had gone off to fight in the Napoleonic wars and had never returned. A fourth son, a clerk in Glasgow, had been captured by a press gang and taken aboard a British navy ship, where he had been forced to work until he died on board several months later when the ship was in the Mediterranean Sea. Neil Livingstone, David's father, was the only one of the five sons left alive. Grandpa Livingstone had good reason to fear his grandchildren's leaving the village where they had been born and raised.

Still, the more David thought and prayed about it, the more he felt God was calling him to be a medical missionary. As outrageous as it seemed, the idea would not go away. David discussed it with his pastor and his parents. Although they all thought he had the intelligence to be a doctor and the determination and faith to be a missionary, all three of them shook their heads and told David there was no practical way it would happen. David, however, would not give up. The tiny seed that had been planted in him when he heard Dr. Gutzlaff's letter had grown within him. David knew he would burst if he did not find a way to go to medical school.

One night David sat on his bed in the family's one-room apartment while his sisters Janet and Agnes sat at the table. Thirteen-year-old Janet was playing schoolteacher, quizzing eight-year-old Agnes on English grammar rules for a test at school the next day. As the two girls worked away, David wrote some numbers on a scrap of paper. He looked at them. Twelve pounds. It would cost twelve pounds to attend Anderson College in Glasgow for a term. Anderson College was the least expensive college David had been able to find that offered courses in basic medicine. David would need another twelve pounds for lodging, food, and books. The numbers he had written down revealed the depressing truth. David now made five shillings a week working as a spinner in the mill. Since there were twenty shillings in a pound, he earned one pound a month. He ran his hands over his face. If he saved every penny he earned, it would take him an entire year to have enough money to pay for one term of college. But of course, he could not do that. He had to buy his own clothes and help pay for both the rent and Charles, Janet, and Agnes's schooling. On top of that, he helped to buy food for the family and gave generously to the church. He jotted down some more calculations. Three years. If he saved every extra penny he could, in three years he would have enough money saved to attend medical school for one term. By then he would be twenty-three years old.

David looked up from his calculations. They were not discouraging; rather, they gave him hope.

It could be done. It might take a while, but with
some determination and hard work, he would go to
medical school and then on to China as a missionary. He had made up his mind. Nothing was going
to stop him now!

When David told his parents of his plans, they
doubted he could save that much money. Surely,
they argued, he would change his mind before three
years were up. Some girl would come along, and
like his older brother John, he would settle down
with a wife to raise a family right in Blantyre. But
David was determined, and in November 1836, he
had finally saved enough money to go to Anderson
College. Not only that, he had not had a single girl-
friend in the entire three years for fear the tempta-
tion to get married would stop him from reaching
his goal.

It was a cold, snowy morning when David and
his father set out together on the eight-mile walk to
Glasgow. Between them they carried everything
David would need for five months: a change of
clothes, several hand-sewn notebooks, a plate and
cup, a bone spoon, and a woolen blanket. In his
pocket David had twenty pounds and the addresses
of some cheap boarding houses where a friend had
told him he might be able to rent a room.

After two and a half hours of walking, David and
his father reached the outskirts of Glasgow, marked
by row upon row of dreary red brick tenement
houses stretching as far as the eye could see. It was
unlike anything David had experienced in Blantyre,

and for a while he walked alongside his father silent and wide-eyed. Together they trudged from one address to the next, but even the cheapest boarding houses were too expensive for David. Finally, one landlady told David that if he could afford to pay only two shillings a week for a room, there was only one place in Glasgow for him—Rotten Row!

Rotten Row certainly did not sound like an appealing place to live, but David and his father followed the landlady's directions and soon found themselves standing in front of a dilapidated wooden building. Several babies were crying loudly inside, and a woman was yelling at the top of her voice. David knocked gingerly on the well-worn door.

"It's not locked," came a reply from inside.

David turned the knob, and he and his father entered a dingy, candlelit hallway.

"Well, what is it you'd be wanting then?" asked a stout older woman with a dirty apron tied around her waist.

"Do you have a room I could rent?" asked David, looking around the dusty hallway.

"I only have one," replied the woman, "upstairs, second on the right. It has a bed and a chair in it. The bathroom is out the back door, and I'll give you a cupboard in the kitchen to keep your food. Now how does that sound for two shillings a week, eh? A bargain I'd say."

David sighed. Even without seeing the bedroom, he knew it was hardly a bargain, but it was a roof over his head and a place to keep his books. "I'll take it," he said.

"That will be four shillings," said the woman shrewdly, "two for the first week's rent and two for a deposit."

"I'll put my things upstairs and bring the money down in a moment," said David, picking up his bag and heading for the stairs.

The room was every bit as bad as he had imagined it would be. Mold grew on the inside of the walls, and there wasn't enough space in the room for David and his father to step inside and shut the door. It took only a moment for David to put his things away.

"Well, God bless you, lad," said Mr. Livingstone. "You know we'll do whatever we can for you. And we want you to come home whenever you can spare the time." With that he shook his son's hand and began the walk back to Blantyre.

David stood on the doorstep and watched his father disappear around the corner of the building. For the first time in his life, twenty-three-year-old David Livingstone felt completely alone. He had never spent a single night away from home before, and he had always had his brothers and sisters and parents and grandparents around him. For a brief moment, he wanted to run after his father, but he had worked and saved for medical school too long to turn back now.

Impossible as it was to believe, the bed in David's tiny room was even more uncomfortable than it looked, and David was glad to climb out of it early the following morning. A big day lay ahead of him. By mail he had enrolled in chemistry, medical Greek, and religion classes, but now it was time to meet his professors and fellow students.

David would never forget his first weeks of study at Anderson College. He woke up every morning with the excitement of going on a new adventure, an adventure in learning. Until now all of his schooling had been done after a long day of work at the mill. Now he could study in the morning and afternoon when his mind was fresh. What a change it was to be able to read and take notes without forcing himself to stay awake! He had read his textbooks through from cover to cover long before his professors were finished introducing their courses, and he stayed long after class debating what he had learned with the other students. For the first time, David felt he was mixing with people who valued learning as much as he did.

Most of David's fellow students had attended the best schools in England in preparation for college, and their fathers were paying for their tuition at Anderson College. Despite the fact that David came from a low social class, the other students quickly accepted him as a fellow student. His interest and enthusiasm more than made up for his lack of a "correct" social background.

The whole college atmosphere made David feel more alive than he had felt in his entire life. Despite his living conditions at Rotten Row and the nights when he had nothing more to eat than a bowl of cold porridge, he never doubted he was in the right place. Of course, it helped that Anderson College buzzed with the latest scientific discoveries, especially in the new area of electricity. Two of the senior students had constructed a galvanic battery and now had enough current to perform a number of electrical experiments.

While all this interested David, the thing that fascinated him the most was learning to treat sickness. David never lost sight of his goal of being a missionary to China. He took notes in class on all of the latest medical techniques, such as how long to bloodlet a person for varying illnesses, the exact number of leeches to use to suck blood, and the quickest way to amputate an injured person's limb. He also learned how to use a new gadget called a stethoscope, which allowed a doctor for the first time to hear air and blood flowing inside the human body.

All these new advances fascinated David's family, too. Mr. Livingstone had changed his mind completely about science and religion being incompatible. Now that he realized that science could help spread the gospel message, he was eager to hear about all David was learning, as was the rest of the family. Once a month, David would make the sixteen-mile round-trip home to Blantyre, where his father would throw an extra log on the fire and his mother would brew a large pot of tea as the entire family gathered to listen with rapt attention as he described life in Glasgow and the wonders of medical science.

These conversations fired David's younger brother and sisters' imaginations and opened their minds to other possibilities besides working in the mills. His sisters, Janet and Agnes, decided to work hard to become schoolteachers, while Charles made up his mind to study to become a pastor.

In April 1837, five months after arriving in Glasgow, David had completed his first term at college. He had also run out of money, and so he left his room on Rotten Row and returned to Blantyre to work in the cotton mill and save more money so he could go back to college the following November.

It felt strange to David to be back working in the mill after mixing with such well-educated people all winter. While his hands worked the loom David thought about the new courses he planned to take during his next term at Anderson College.

Even though David worked hard and saved every penny he could, when it came time to return to college, he did not have enough to go back. But before he could despair, his older brother John, who now had a respectable job as a lace merchant, offered to give David the money he needed. It was the old Scottish way: David had helped his younger siblings, and now he was receiving help from his older brother when he needed it most. He was truly grateful.

David's next term at college was just as exciting as his first. David had a mind like a sponge, and he wanted to learn all he could about everything. He made friends with a professor's assistant named James Young. James had been hired to make science equipment to use for experiments, and David was fascinated by his workshop. James taught David how to use a lathe to turn wood and a furnace to heat glass and metal. David also learned how to mend broken or damaged pieces of science equipment. After all, David reasoned, since he had no way of predicting what he would be called upon to do once he was a missionary in China, he wanted to learn as much as possible.

Chapter 4

He Had No Answers

David Livingstone sat quietly in the library at Anderson College. In front of him was an application to join the London Missionary Society (LMS) to work in China. The question he was pondering was, "What do you see as the most important work of a missionary?" It was a question David had given much thought to since returning to college for his second term. But how should he put his thoughts into words? Finally it came to him: "The missionary's object is to endeavor by every means in his power to make known the gospel by preaching, exhortation, conversation, instruction of the young; improving, so far as is in his power, the temporal condition of those among whom he labors, by introducing the arts and sciences to civilization, and doing everything to commend Christianity to their hearts and consciences."

David read over his answer with satisfaction. Yes, that was what a missionary was—a person who told other people about the gospel message at the same time that he worked to improve their lives in every way possible. However, David had read enough missionary stories to know that the people a missionary tried to help did not always appreciate their effort. So he went on and wrote, "The missionary will be exposed to great trials of his faith and patience from the indifference, distrust, and even direct opposition and scorn of those for whose good he is laboring."

It took David all afternoon to finish the questions, but in the end, he was satisfied he had told the LMS all it wanted to know about him. He placed the completed application in an envelope and mailed it to London.

David did not have to wait long for a reply. When it arrived, he ripped open the envelope bearing the insignia of the London Missionary Society and quickly scanned the contents of the letter inside. The letter read: "The London Missionary Society has received and reviewed your application and is happy to inform you that you have been provisionally accepted for our missionary training program. However, the course you have chosen is a rigorous one and you will need to apply consistent effort and diligence if you are to achieve your goal of being sent out as a missionary with our society."

Other people might drop out, David thought to himself as he read, *but not me. I'll never be tempted to do that.*

In September 1838, David completed his course of study at Anderson College. Much to his amazement, he was offered a job as a teacher at the college at a salary of 150 pounds a year—a small fortune to a twenty-five-year-old who had spent over half his life laboring in a cotton mill for twelve pounds a year. But the money did not tempt David, who stayed true to his word. David had set his heart on being a missionary, with all the trials, tribulations, and lack of funds that it entailed.

At the end of his time at Anderson College, David packed up his few belongings and caught a stagecoach to London to meet with the directors of the London Missionary Society. After a long and bumpy journey, the coach finally pulled to a halt in London. David stared around him in awe. Hard as it was to believe, he really was in London, four hundred miles from Glasgow!

By asking passersby for directions, David was able to find his way to 57 Aldersgate Street, where the LMS had told him he could find cheap lodgings. That night he sat down to dinner with the four other lodgers. One was a young doctor; one a saddle maker; another, a fellow Scot, was a bookseller. The fourth was a young man who introduced himself as Joseph Moore. Before David had finished his first bowl of soup, he and Joseph had struck up a conversation. What a relief it was for David to learn that Joseph Moore had also come to London that day to meet with the directors of the London Missionary Society. Now David did not feel so over-whelmed by all that lay ahead. He had made his first friend in London.

The next morning, Wednesday, David and Joseph Moore met for breakfast and decided to spend the day together. The first thing they did was visit the London Missionary Society offices, where they were told to report the following Monday and Tuesday mornings to take Latin, Greek, and theology examinations. David was nervous as he left the office. He was a good student, but Joseph had already told him about several of his friends who had not managed to pass the tough exams.

To take their minds off what lay ahead, the two young men set out to see the sights of London. They strolled past Buckingham Palace, where a flag indicated that newly crowned Queen Victoria was in residence. They strolled across London Bridge and passed the Tower of London. On Sunday they went to three different churches. There were so many wonderful sermons to hear in such a large city.

David tried to remember every detail of what he saw so that he could write home and tell his family all about London. He pictured them all sitting around the fire reading his letters and trying to imagine what life was like in such a faraway place.

On Monday morning, David and Joseph Moore took their first exam. Afterwards they walked to

Westminster Abbey, where they looked at the graves of Great Britain's most famous people who had been honored by being buried within the Abbey. Little did David know that one day he too would be one of the famous people buried there.

After the second exam on Tuesday morning, both men were interviewed by the directors of the London Missionary Society. Much to David's relief, both he and Joseph Moore had passed their exams and were officially accepted into the training program. One of the directors explained that they would study for three months under the guidance of the Reverend Richard Cecil, who lived in Chipping Ongar, a small town in Essex. If at the end of that time the Reverend Cecil recommended them as good students, Joseph would go on to further theological training and David to further medical training as the final stage in their preparation to become missionaries. This pleased David greatly. Although he had learned a lot of medical theory while at Anderson College, David hadn't spent much time treating patients. He looked forward to the opportunity to diagnose diseases and operate on people.

Life at Chipping Ongar was harder than David had anticipated. The Reverend Cecil seemed to not care much for Scottish people. He criticized David's strong accent, nor did he have many kind words to say about David's Latin and Greek. The Reverend Cecil was a hard taskmaster, but with great effort, David was able to complete the work he was given. That is, until one Sunday.

David heard a knock at the door of the boarding house where he was staying. Then he heard the landlady call his name. "Mr. Livingstone," she said, "there is a messenger boy here for you."

David hurried from the parlor into the boarding house entrance, where he found the Reverend Cecil's houseboy. "A letter for you, sir," said the houseboy, handing the sealed envelope to David.

"Thank you," replied David, wondering what the Reverend Cecil had to say to him that couldn't wait until the following day.

David unfolded the letter and read it. "Dear Mr. Livingstone, the minister at Stamford Rivers has sent word to me that he is ill and will not be able to preach tonight. I would like you to take his place. The service begins at 6 P.M., and you will need to be there at 5 P.M. Thank you. Sincerely, Reverend R. Cecil."

David read the letter through again. He looked at the clock on the mantel. It would take him an hour to walk to Stamford Rivers. Thankfully, he already had a sermon written and memorized. Learning to write good sermons was one of the requirements for missionaries in training. David found this requirement one of the easier things he'd had to do in the training course. He liked to make his thoughts flow logically, and he had a wonderful memory. And even though he had not been expecting to preach his first sermon at such short notice, he was not concerned about it.

Four hours later David was standing in front of the modest-sized congregation. As the strains of the final verse of the hymn faded, David knew it was time to deliver his sermon. He walked confidently to the pulpit and looked out at the congregation. He could hardly believe his eyes! There, right in the front row, sat the Reverend Cecil. A million thoughts suddenly raced through David's mind. He had to remember not to speak in his Scottish accent. He had to pause between the first and second parts of his sermon to allow the congregation a moment to reflect. He had to remember to raise his voice on the last sentence and look directly at the congregation.

The church was silent as everyone waited for David to begin. But the man who had been able to recite Psalm 119 since he was nine years old could suddenly not remember a single word of his sermon. He stood in the pulpit for a full minute waiting for the first line of the sermon to come to him, but it did not. The Reverend Cecil's steely blue eyes settled firmly on David as if to say, "Ah ha! I knew you couldn't do it."

David opened his mouth. "Friends," he began calmly, and then, unable to come up with anything else intelligent to say, he blurted, "I have forgotten all I had to say." With that he slammed his Bible shut, tucked it under his arm, and raced down the aisle and out the front door of the church. He never looked back until he was safely in his room at the boarding house with the door shut firmly behind him.

David sat on the edge of his bed, scarcely able to believe what he had just done. Of course, the whole sermon came flooding back to his mind soon after he walked out of the church, but it was too late. He was certain that as a result of this incident, he had just failed the training course with the Reverend Cecil. He was right.

The next morning the Reverend Cecil called David into his office. "As you know," he began in a droning voice, "a large part of being a missionary is the ability to prepare and preach an adequate sermon. Last night you proved you were not able to do that, and although you have passed the other aspects of the course, I cannot recommend you to the London Missionary Society for further study. I have nothing more to say."

As David walked back to the boarding house, he was grateful that the Reverend Cecil had kept his remarks short. The last thing he wanted was to relive the humiliation of the night before!

"It's over," David said gloomily to Joseph Moore as the two of them took an afternoon stroll together. But he was so caught up in his own thoughts and feelings that he hadn't noticed how depressed Joseph was.

"I know," said Joseph Moore. "Me too."

David stopped and looked at his friend. "What do you mean?" he asked.

Joseph looked at the ground as he spoke. "Reverend Cecil has failed me too. He says my marks in Hebrew are not good enough."

"I'm sorry. What happens now?" asked David.

The question hung in the chilly afternoon air. David had never seriously considered that he would fail the probationary course. He had always been an excellent student, and although he would be the first to admit he was not a gripping speaker, he had assumed he would be able to preach an adequate sermon. How wrong he had been!

The two friends continued in their gloom for two more days until the Reverend Cecil summoned them both back to his office with good news. Although he had recommended that David and Joseph Moore not continue with the mission, the LMS directors had not accepted his recommendation. Instead, they wanted to give both men a second chance and had extended their probationary period for another three months so that Joseph could work on his Hebrew and David on his preaching.

David was glad to have a second chance, though he doubted he would ever please the Reverend Cecil. However, he didn't flee from the church the next time he was asked to preach, and by the end of the three months, both he and Joseph Moore had passed the course. Joseph went on to Cheshunt College, where he continued studying theology in preparation for missionary work in Tahiti in the South Pacific Ocean. David was invited back to London to continue his medical studies at Charing Cross Hospital under the watchful eye of Dr. Bennett.

David knew he still had a lot to learn about practical medicine, particularly about operating on people. Until this time all the "surgery" he had performed had been on dead corpses, or cadavers, as the bodies medical students practiced on were called. He soon found that operating on a live body was quite different from operating on a dead one. For one thing, the live person flinched and recoiled from the pain of being cut and poked and prodded!

Under the guidance of Professor Owen at the Hunterian Museum, David studied the similarities and differences between humans and animals. He and Professor Owen struck up a strong friendship, and David promised that if he ever found anything interesting on his travels he would be sure to send it back to the professor for display in the museum.

When he was not studying, David was out and about in London, taking in all the sights and sounds the bustling city had to offer. He attended a meeting at Exeter Hall, where Queen Victoria's new husband, Prince Albert, gave his first speech in England. It was a grand occasion, a ceremony to send off the Niger Expedition, which was going to explore a remote area of West Africa. Robert Moffat, a tall, imposing missionary to southern Africa, also spoke at the meeting.

The gathering fired David Livingstone with new enthusiasm to get to the mission field. There was so much work to do. There was just one problem: The British were at war with China over trading restrictions. In 1839, Great Britain had sold forty thousand cases of opium in China. The opium, a very addictive drug, was produced from a special breed of poppies grown in India. The Chinese emperor was furious that a foreign power would dare to sell something as destructive as opium to his people and ordered the British to stop at once. But since a great profit was being made selling the opium in China, the British refused to obey the emperor's order. As a result, a war broke out between the British and the Chinese. It was called the Opium War, and it was still raging as David Livingstone was making final preparations to set sail for China. All David had left to do was return to Glasgow and take his physician's examination to qualify as a doctor. However, since a war was raging in China, the London Missionary Society decided it would send no more missionaries to China until peace and calm had returned. The trouble was, no one could predict when that would be, so the London Missionary Society suggested that David go to the West Indies as a missionary once he had qualified as a doctor.

The West Indies, though, was not where David wanted to go. All the mission stations there were well established, and David would be expected to work alongside a large group of other missionaries and practice medicine in a hospital. Although he got along well with others, David had set his mind on being a pioneer missionary. He wanted to walk where no other missionary had walked, treat people who had never seen a European doctor, and preach to those who had never heard the gospel message. The West Indies might be a fine place for other missionaries, but it was not what David Livingstone had in mind. David knew he was a leader, not a follower, and he told the directors of the London Missionary Society so. But when the directors asked him where he would like to go, he had no answer.

Chapter 5

The Smoke of a Thousand Villages

D avid Livingstone sat at the dinner table in the Aldersgate Street boarding house where he was staying. Seated opposite him was the Reverend Robert Moffat, the missionary he had heard speak at Exeter Hall with Prince Albert. The Reverend Moffat was a missionary in southern Africa and was making his first trip home with his family in twenty years. He was staying in the boarding house while in London to meet with the directors of the London Missionary Society. David had been a little confused by some of the things the Reverend Moffat had said at the meeting in Exeter Hall. He decided to ask him for some clarification.

"Reverend Moffat," he began, "all I have read about Africa would lead me to believe that it is populated only around the edges, that the middle is a huge, unpopulated wilderness. Yet you speak as if there are people living deep inland as well as on the coast. What makes you think that?"

The Reverend Moffat put down his fork and began to speak in his strong Scottish accent, which hadn't diminished one bit despite all his years in Africa. "I don't think it, laddie, I know it. I know the popular view is that the center of Africa is a wasteland, but that's only because no white man has ventured inland. But I can tell you this, some mornings I have got up and looked towards the vast plain to the north and seen the smoke of a thousand villages where no missionary has ever been!" His eyes gleamed with excitement as he spoke.

David sat silent for a moment, taking in the enormity of what the older missionary had just told him. Africa was not empty after all. It was filled with people, people who needed to hear the gospel message.

Before David had finished his mutton stew, he had made up his mind. He would not wait for the end of the Opium War in China. There was missionary work to be done in Africa. That's where he would go.

It took several letters to the directors of the London Missionary Society for David to convince them that Africa was the right place for him. The directors were reluctant to send an inexperienced missionary to Africa, which they considered a dark and dangerous place. Indeed, the continent had been nicknamed the "white man's graveyard." Still, David's persistence paid off, and David was given permission to go to Africa—on one condition. After he had qualified as a doctor, he would need to be ordained as a minister.

David returned to Glasgow in November 1840 to take his physician's exams, which he passed with flying colors. His family was very proud of the new "Dr. Livingstone" when he returned to Shuttle Row in Blantyre to visit. David was proud of them all, too. By now his oldest brother John's lace business was booming, while younger brother Charles had emigrated to the United States and was studying to become a pastor at Oberlin College in Ohio. His sisters were also doing well. Both Janet and Agnes were teachers at a local school. With hard work and education, each of his brothers and sisters had managed to escape a lifetime of drudgery working in the cotton mills.

David could spend only one night at home with his parents. He was expected back in London for his ordination ceremony at the Albion Street Chapel in four days. That autumn night the Livingstone family sat up talking late into the evening. David told his parents and sisters all about London and all he knew about Africa. Just before David had left for Glasgow, the London Missionary Society had sent a letter to him informing him he had been assigned to work at the Reverend Moffat's mission station at Kuruman.

Despite the late night of talking, David awoke in the morning at five o'clock. The rich aroma of

brewing coffee rather than the tea the family nor-
mally drank filled the apartment. David's mother
and father were already up and dressed. David
folded the blanket he had slept under on the
wooden floor and put it away, then sat down with
his father to a bowl of hot porridge. It wasn't long
before Janet and Agnes joined them.

"David, how far is Kuruman from the coast?"
asked Agnes.

"It's about six hundred miles inland, and almost
due north from Port Elizabeth in southern Africa,"
he replied.

"You will remember to write, won't you?" asked
Janet anxiously. "I love the letters you send from
London. When people at church ask me what you're
doing and how they can pray for you, I know what
to tell them."

"I'll write," promised David, "though it's going
to take three or four months for a letter to get from
the coast of Africa to Scotland. If I go inland, goodness knows how long it will take to hear from me."

"Well, if we don't hear from you for a while,
we'll just pray all the more," smiled his mother
bravely as she poured David another cup of coffee.
"Now tell me, what are you going to take with you?
Is there anything you need?"

David smiled back at his mother. Even though
he was now twenty-seven years old, she still liked
to fuss over him. "According to Reverend Moffat,
I'll be able to buy most of the supplies I'll need in
Port Elizabeth before heading inland," he said.

"Would you take the morning Bible reading for us before you go?" Mr. Livingstone asked his son, handing him the black leather-bound family Bible.

David took the familiar book in both hands, as he had done so many times before. He flicked the Bible open to Psalm 121, his favorite psalm, and began to read. "I will lift up mine eyes unto the hills, from whence cometh my help. My help cometh from the Lord, which made heaven and earth."

The final words of the psalm, "The Lord shall preserve thy going out and thy coming in from this time forth, and even for evermore," were still echoing in David's mind as he set out with his father to walk to Glasgow to catch the boat to Liverpool, from where he would take a coach to London. As father and son walked along together in the still morning air, David wondered whether this was the last hour he would ever spend with his father. Neil Livingstone was fifty-two years old and did not look well. And although his father would not complain about his health, David noticed he didn't have the same spring in his step as when he'd accompanied David to Glasgow to attend Anderson College four years before.

It was a sad parting in Glasgow for David and his father. Mr. Livingstone's health was failing, and David was on his way to the white man's grave. Neither of them expected to see each other again, and David stood on the aft deck for a long time watching his father disappear from view as the boat slipped down the Broomielaw and out to sea.

Two and a half weeks later, on December 8, 1840, the Reverend Doctor David Livingstone stood on the stern of another ship. This time it was the *George*, a sleek three-masted sailing ship under the command of Captain Donaldsen. On board with David were William Ross and his wife, who were also on their way to be missionaries at Kuruman. In fact, William Ross had been ordained in the same ceremony as David two weeks before. Both men were now officially ministers with the London Missionary Society.

David loved life at sea. He enjoyed the sound of the waves crashing against the bow of the ship, and he loved watching the dolphins that swam along-side. He was also fascinated by the stars and the navigation equipment the *George* carried. Captain Donaldsen showed him how to make lunar obser-vations at night with the quadrant and chart the position of the stars on a map. Soon David was as accurate at this as the captain. He did not know it at the time, but it would be a skill he was glad to have in Africa.

The Ross family, however, were not clambering around on deck. William and his wife were both very seasick for almost the entire voyage. David tended to them as best he could, but there was nothing he could do to stop the pitching and rolling of the ship that was the source of their sickness.

With William Ross confined to his cabin, David became responsible for the Sunday service in the dining room. He had high hopes for the service, but once again he was reminded that he was not a natural preacher. The few crew that attended the service were sullen and rude, and David's sermons didn't seem to grab their attention.

The *George* was headed for Port Elizabeth, with a stop in Cape Town on the way. About halfway through the voyage, the ship was lashed by a massive storm. Captain Donaldsen's stubborn determination kept the ship afloat, but when the storm finally subsided, the *George* had lost her main mast and most of her sails. As a result, she was at the mercy of the currents and the trade winds, which were pushing her westward towards South America. As the ship drifted helplessly across the Atlantic Ocean, David noticed a marked increase in attendance at the Sunday service, and the crew became much quieter and better behaved.

David watched each night as Captain Donaldsen took quadrant readings and plotted their new position. Each day they moved closer and closer to South America until they finally spotted land dead ahead. They were just off Rio de Janeiro, Brazil, five thousand miles and a continent away from their destination.

Still, Brazil was a mission field. Although it was not the mission field to which he had been assigned, David was eager to begin some missionary work. He unpacked a number of tracts and Bibles and disembarked the ship as soon as it docked in Rio de Janeiro. Captain Donaldsen told him it would take about a week for emergency repairs to be made to the ship so that it could make its way back across the Atlantic Ocean to Cape Town. David invited William Ross to accompany him, but William felt too weak from all the seasickness. Besides, William protested, he'd signed up to be a missionary to Africa, not South America.

Undeterred, David walked for many miles, talking to people and handing out tracts and Bibles. He visited many pubs and bars to talk to sailors about the gospel message. He was appalled by what he saw in these places. The sailors were usually drunk and out of control, and the worst-behaved of them all were the British sailors. Because they set such a bad example for the local people, David was embarrassed to be from the same country as they.

A week later, the *George* had new sails flapping from her remaining masts, and the broken railings and hatch covers had been repaired. The ship was soon headed east across the Atlantic Ocean towards southern Africa. They encountered no more storms to push them off course, and in early March 1841, the *George* arrived at Simon's Bay off Cape Town. Of course, because of the detour to South America, they arrived much later than expected. And they would be even later getting to Port Elizabeth because the ship was to undergo an overhaul and have a new main mast fitted in Cape Town. This would leave the three missionaries stranded in Cape Town for a month while the work on the ship was carried out.

During their stay in Cape Town, David and the Rosses were guests at the London Missionary Society station there. David made himself as useful as he could, but after only a few days he was restless. He was finally in Africa, but there was a whole unexplored continent to the north of him, and he was itching to see it all. The smoke of a thousand villages beckoned him to get moving inland. By contrast, William Ross and his wife were very glad to spend the month in Cape Town. After the crowded conditions of the ship, living at the mission station seemed blissful for them. They began to wonder whether God had really called them inland. After all, there was a lot of work to be done on the coast.

William Ross discussed his feelings with David, who was astonished that any missionary would consider staying on the coast when there was so much work to be done inland. Secretly, he labeled men like William Ross "veranda missionaries"— people who didn't really want to leave their front porch to venture out into the mission field. Indeed, since boarding the *George*, William Ross and his wife had done nothing but complain about how bad things were. David had tried to overlook their complaining because they were so sick. But now that the Rosses were having second thoughts about whether they should even be going inland as missionaries, their behavior irritated David. David began to wonder how he would ever work alongside William Ross at Kuruman. He was already sick of hearing from him about how much better things were in England. When an opening for a pastor came up in Cape Town, David privately hoped that William Ross would take the job. But much to

David's chagrin, William did not, and on April 15, 1841, all three missionaries set sail aboard the refitted *George* on the final leg of their sea voyage to Port Elizabeth.

Chapter 6

Kuruman at Last

So, how much do you want for it?" asked David Livingstone as he walked around the wagon.

"That's hard to say," responded the trader wearing a tattered cloth hat. "A wagon like this is in big demand, what with the Boers and their trek north."

David nodded. He had heard all about the Dutch settlers, or Boers as they were called, who had headed up into the land of the Zulus in the northeast to get away from the British who dominated the coastline of southern Africa.

"I'll give you forty pounds for it, and not a penny more," said David, feeling for the purse in his coat pocket.

"Fifty and it's yours, and that's as low as I'll go," replied the trader.

David looked around. No other wagons were in sight, and this was a particularly large one. It would need twelve oxen to pull it, but it should carry more than enough supplies for three missionaries and three native guides. "Done," he finally said. "I'll give you half the money now and the other half when I come back with the oxen. My partner should be buying them right now."

The trader nodded. "So you're headed north, are you?" he asked. "But not to join the Boers. You have a Scottish accent if I'm not mistaken."

"That's right. Glasgow, in fact. I'm headed up to Kuruman to the mission station," responded David.

"Ha," replied the trader, wiping his brow with a dusty handkerchief. "So you're a missionary, are you? Well, you watch yourself heading that way. It's not as safe as it used to be up there. The Boers have moved in to the Zulus' land. It was guns against spears, and the Zulus couldn't keep them out. Now the Zulus have moved down closer to the coast, pushing other tribes off their lands. This struggle between the Zulus and the Boers is a pot waiting to boil over, you mark my words. The English think they've got rid of the Boers, but no good will come of them taking land from the natives." He pointed his finger at David and then added, "Just mind you don't get stuck in the middle of it. It'll be a nasty business when it blows up."

David nodded. He had heard a lot about the Boers and their trek into the hinterland of southern Africa. And while he admired their determination and courage, he could not agree with the way they had settled land already belonging to African tribes. What the trader had said made perfect sense. It would be only a matter of time before hatred of the Boers turned into widespread bloodshed. "Thank you for the advice. I'll be back soon," David finally said to the trader, handing him twenty-five pounds.

David walked a little farther along the rambling street that was transformed into a market every Wednesday morning. This was the third week in a row he and William Ross had come looking for a wagon and oxen. Getting supplies together for the trip to Kuruman had taken five times longer than David had imagined it would. Still, at least they now had a wagon.

"Over here," called William Ross. "What do you think of these?"

David looked in the direction from which William Ross was beckoning. Tied to a post were three of the toughest-looking oxen he had ever seen. They were unlike any animal David had encountered in Scotland. They were bulky, mean-looking animals with curled horns that lay flat against the back of their neck.

"The owner says there are twelve of them," said William. "What do you think?"

"They look fine to me," said David, "as long as they're all that big and healthy. How much does he want for them?"

"Three pounds each," replied William Ross.

"Then let's buy them," said David. "I've found a wagon that will do fine, and it needs a dozen oxen to pull it. It looks like we're in business at last! At the rate we were going I thought we might be stuck here till spring." David grinned to himself as he spoke. Finally things were coming together.

The two missionaries returned with the wagon and oxen to the boarding house where they were staying in Port Elizabeth. It took them two more days to gather all the supplies they would need for the journey north. The Reverend Moffat had told David it would take about two months to get to Kuruman, so they made sure they bought enough food for the trip. They loaded cheese, salt bacon, coffee, tea, beans, flour, and sugar into the wagon. They also purchased cots to sleep on. The Rosses were going to sling theirs inside the wagon, while David would use a small one-man tent.

Finally, on the morning of May 15, 1841, the group was ready to leave Port Elizabeth. David couldn't wait to get away from all signs of civilization and out into the wilds of Africa. Within an hour, he had his wish. Port Elizabeth was behind them, and in every direction was spread the vastness of the African continent. The three Africans they had hired to guide them walked alongside the wagon, pointing out interesting things and giving the Bantu names for antelope, gazelle, giraffe, and water buffalo.

Africa was all David Livingstone had imagined it would be—and more. The tall grasses, the fantastically shaped trees, the pink-tinged hills in the distance. David felt that this was what he had been born for. When they made camp on the third night, he wrote in his journal, "I like traveling very much indeed. There is so much freedom connected with our African manners. We pitch our tent, make our fire, etc., wherever we choose, walk, ride, or shoot an abundance of all sorts of game as our inclination leads us; but there is a great drawback: we can't study or read when we please."

The reason David couldn't study and read when he pleased was that he had left the wagon for the Rosses to fuss around in. Since he could no longer stand their complaining, he either walked along with the African guides or rode one of the oxen pulling the wagon. Of course, this made it impossible for him to read or study, which he could have done had he been riding in the wagon. Still, it was better than listening to the complaints of his two companions day in and day out.

The group crossed several large rivers on the journey, including the Orange River, which caused a fresh outburst of panic from Mrs. Ross. As David clambered into the chest-deep water to soothe the oxen and lead them to the other side, he again wondered how he was ever going to get along with these "veranda missionaries."

Progress was slow on the trip. Kuruman was six hundred miles from Port Elizabeth, and they were covering about ten miles a day over the rocky ground. Thankfully, it was winter—the dry season—with no rain to make the journey any slower. Gradually they ate their way through their food supplies. They supplemented this food with the wild game David shot, providing them with many delicious dinners along the way. Every hundred miles or so they passed through a mission station. First there was Somerset East, then Colesburg, Phillipolis, and Griqua Town. At each mission station, they were welcomed and given what food and drink could be spared to take with them on their journey.

As they got closer to Kuruman, the landscape began to change. There were fewer trees now, and more thorny bushes. The riverbeds were dry, and the air was thinner, since they were climbing steadily from one plateau to the next as they moved farther inland. Seated at the campfire at night, David tried to write about everything he saw. He collected samples to send back to his friend, Professor Owen, at the Hunterian Museum in London. He wished he could describe more fully what he was seeing. No naturalists had ventured this far inland into Africa, and David tried his best to help Professor Owen understand the wonders of the landscape. Everywhere he looked he saw something he had never seen before, never even dreamed of. Snakes slithered from behind rocks, scorpions scuttled around in the dust, wildly colored spiders wove impossibly big webs outside his tent at night, and armies of ants carried off any food foolishly left unattended.

Eventually, on July 31, 1841, David Livingstone caught his first sight of Kuruman, the most inland missionary station in Africa. Kuruman had been established by the Reverend Moffat almost twenty years before. Of course, the Reverend Moffat and his family were not back from furlough yet, but the group was given an enthusiastic welcome in Kuruman by the missionaries living there—Roger Edwards and his wife and Robert Hamilton. Within an hour of arriving, the wagon had been unloaded and the oxen led away to be watered. David and the Rosses soon found themselves seated at a table on the veranda of the main mission house. Mrs. Edwards, a motherly woman in her late forties, busied herself, bringing tea and sandwiches and chattering with Mrs. Ross. David and William Ross produced newspapers and letters from Port Elizabeth. The papers were nearly three months old by now, but they were the latest news available to the missionaries at Kuruman.

After Roger Edwards and Robert Hamilton had looked over the newspapers and read some of the letters, the conversation turned to the mission compound and life in Kuruman.

"Let's leave the ladies here to discuss the fineries of African fashion," said Roger Edwards, jumping to his feet. "I'll show you around the compound."

The four men stepped off the veranda.

"I'll show you the church first. It's over this way," said Roger, moving to the front of the group.

As they rounded the corner of the mission house, David was awed by the huge, mud brick building he saw. "Is that the church?" he asked, thinking how much bigger and better it was compared to the churches at the other mission stations they had passed through along the way.

"It certainly is," replied Roger. "We have over four hundred natives here every Sunday."

"Amazing," said David. "To think there are four hundred Christian men and women out here in the middle of Africa."

"Well, I wouldn't say they are all Christians," said Roger, who paused and looked down at the ground for a moment before continuing. "Actually, only about forty of them are really Christians, that's if you mean people who have been baptized and follow the teachings of the church."

"Oh," said David. "Forty Christians? You don't mean there are only forty Christians in the whole of Kuruman, do you?"

"I'm afraid so. It's not as easy as you might think converting the natives. They have their own ways of doing things, you know," defended Roger Edwards.

David was too stunned to ask any more questions for the moment. Twenty years and only forty converts!

"Look over here," cut in Robert Hamilton brightly, changing the subject. "This is one of our best projects yet—an irrigation system."

David's eyes lit up. Engineering was something he could appreciate. The four men walked on past the church to where many acres of lush land stretched eastward. It looked exactly the way David had always imagined the Garden of Eden to look. Huge flower bushes and vegetables plants vied for space in the sun. The branches of orange and lemon trees dipped low under the weight of their fruit.

Color and life were everywhere. And running through the middle of it all were ditches flowing with fresh, cold water.

"Where does the water come from?" asked David.

"The Eye of Kuruman. That's what we call the spring," said Robert Hamilton, adding, "It's one of the best springs around, too."

The men traced the irrigation ditches back to the enormous gushing spring. On the way they passed blacksmith and carpentry workshops. David peeked inside the carpentry shop, where he found everything laid out in perfect order. The rasps and screwdrivers were arranged in descending order, and there was a small wood lathe in the corner. David thought back to the hours he had spent learning to turn wood on the lathe in the workshop at Anderson College. He might be able to put those skills to work in Kuruman.

The sun was going down in a spectacular blaze of red as the men returned to the table on the veranda for another cup of tea. Mrs. Ross was happier than David had ever seen her. She was gushing praise for the china tea set they were drinking from and asking Mrs. Edwards endless questions about the cost of food and what the servants could and could not cook.

After drinking the tea, David was glad to get away from all the chatter and into the quiet of his own room. As he shut the door behind him, he realized it was the first time he'd been alone for weeks. He sat on the end of his bed and hauled his bag up beside him. He unbuckled it and reached inside to pull out his journal. Balancing a bottle of India ink on the edge of the bed, he dipped his nib. But what should he write? Should he write about meeting the Edwardses and Robert Hamilton? Or what about his first impressions of Kuruman, with the irrigation system, well-constructed church, and impressive carpentry shop? In the end, he did not write about any of this. Something else was on his mind. He jotted down the number forty.

Ever since David had heard there were only forty practicing Christians in Kuruman, he had been disturbed. He stroked the end of his pen against his cheek and thought about it some more. Many people said that the Reverend Moffat was perhaps the most famous and most successful missionary ever to set foot in Africa. Yet he had converted only forty people in twenty years. That was only two converts per year. David stared at the wall of his small room. He was twenty-eight years old, and he could not hope to become as great a missionary as the Reverend Moffat. But even if he did, he would be forty-eight years old before he had forty converts of his own! The thought horrified David. He had come to Africa to make a difference, to leave a mark, not to stay in one tiny spot with a handful of converts following him around into old age.

Then, to David's surprise, clarity suddenly came to his mind. David realized that living at Kuruman and working with the Reverend Moffat was not for him. The fires of a thousand unmapped and unreached villages were burning to the north of Kuruman, and David had to find some way to reach them. From that moment on, David Livingstone knew that every day he delayed moving north was a day lost.

Chapter 7

Farther North

I'd love to see the plans to expand the irrigation system," said David politely, two mornings after arriving at Kuruman. It was just the chance he had been looking for—a chance to talk privately with Roger Edwards.

As the two men strolled between the rows of cauliflower and corn growing in the garden, David wondered how he should start. Finally, he cleared his throat. "Have you ever thought about going farther north?" he asked.

Roger Edwards looked startled. "Well, I suppose it has crossed my mind from time to time. But there's so much work to be done here I'm not sure the committee in England would think it was a good idea." He looked nervously at David.

"But don't you want to see what's north of here? Kuruman is so small. "There must be much larger settlements not too far away. Hasn't anyone gone to find out where they are?" asked David, pushing the point.

Roger nodded. "Yes, to some extent," he replied. "Reverend Moffat has been to Namaqualand to the west, and he knows the Zulu tribes to the east, but I can't say anyone has gone very far north. A man with the Church Missionary Society went up there for a few months, but he didn't last."

David wasn't sure whether he should go on talking about his plan, but since he sensed some interest, some spirit of adventure in Roger Edwards, he continued. Bending down to examine the rich soil, he said, "I was thinking that perhaps I would take the wagon and oxen and do a little exploring. Would you like to come along?"

"But, but…" Roger was at a loss for words. He took a deep breath before continuing. "What would happen if Reverend Moffat found out? We're meant to follow orders, not just go off and do what we want. I've been here ten years, and Robert Hamilton even longer. Neither of us has ever been told to explore the area north of here."

"I know that," said David soothingly, standing up to face his new friend, "but Reverend Moffat is staying on furlough longer than expected. He'll be away for at least another year. In England we talked about my opening a new mission farther north, but he confessed he didn't know much about the conditions up there. Wouldn't it be good if we had some solid facts to give him when he got back? Perhaps a map with the names of the tribes and chiefs north of here on it, and a list of those who are open to our coming back to work among them. That could only help speed up the whole process."

"But the station here. Who would look after it?" asked Roger.

"That's not a problem," said David. "After all, before we arrived, there were only you and your wife and Robert Hamilton here. If you and I went north, leaving William Ross and his wife behind, there would still be more than enough people to run things here."

Roger laughed nervously. "I see you've thought it all through. I would have thought you'd have been tired of traveling after your journey here, but I see you have traveling in your blood. Let me think about it, David. I must say, it's good to have someone with your enthusiasm here, but it does rock the boat a bit!" With that he patted David on the back. "Come on," he said, "you told me earlier that you were interested in the workshop. Let me show you where we keep the tools."

It was a week before Roger was ready to talk to David about going north. Roger was showing David how to repair a wagon wheel, an essential skill in Africa. As he tapped the spokes into place around the hub he said, "I've been thinking on what you said about going north, and it makes a certain amount of sense to me. There are too many missionaries here right now, and no new work can start until Reverend Moffat gets back. It could be a good idea to gather some facts and have some idea of what lies to the north."

"You mean you'll come with me?" asked David, trying to hide the excitement in his voice.

Roger nodded. "But I won't be able to go until September. I have some translation work I promised to finish by then. You'd better let me handle things with Robert Hamilton, though. I doubt he'll be too enthusiastic about the whole plan."

David floated through the rest of the day. He was going farther north, and soon.

Over the next month, David learned all he could about what lay to the north of Kuruman. Sometimes Bechuana tribesmen would wander into the compound from that direction on their way to the coast. When they did, David or Roger would always question them about what conditions were like from where they had come. From these little pieces of information, David and Roger were able to discover several things. First, the tribe directly to the north of them was the Griquas. Over the past one hundred years, these people had pushed their way inland from the coast. They had many guns and were not afraid to use them on the other tribes around them. Indeed, in moving inland, they had displaced other tribes along the way. One of these tribes was the Bechuana, who had been pushed farther north. Recently, the Griquas had mounted a series of raids on Bechuana villages, and as a result, the village chiefs had become quite hostile to anyone from the outside.

When David heard this, he was more determined than ever to get out among the Bechuana people before they armed themselves with guns and would rather fight than talk. And by the sound of things, he didn't have a moment to lose.

On September 24, 1841, six weeks after David's arrival in Kuruman, the wagon had been over-hauled and restocked and the oxen were well rested. It was time for another adventure. David Living-stone and Roger Edwards, along with an African guide named Pomare and another African Christian, climbed onto the wagon and headed out through the gates of the mission compound. David looked back to see Robert Hamilton and William Ross ner-vously watching them go.

The wagon rumbled along the scrubby bush track that led northward. Once again David was fascinated with the array of wild animals he saw. He wished he were better at drawing, but he did his best to capture with words the way things looked. Herds of rhinoceros and elephants trampled through the bushes, while gazelles and springboks jumped and pranced in the distance, too skittish to allow the men to get close.

It was two weeks before Pomare pointed excit-edly into the distance. "A village," he said. "Over there."

David Livingstone strained for his first look at a Bechuana person. He heard one before he saw one. "Luliloo, luliloo," he heard a woman's voice yelling. He assumed someone had spotted the wagon and was warning the others. Sure enough, within two minutes the ground around the wagon was alive with action. Large black men with glistening bodies, wearing leather tunics and carrying long, sharp spears, jumped and danced around the wagon.

"Are they friendly?" whispered David to Pomare, having no clue how to interpret their behavior.

"I don't think they will hurt us," replied Pomare, "but you must be careful not to show them your gun."

David nodded. The last thing these people needed was to be introduced to deadly weapons as a by-product of hearing the gospel message.

Two of the men from the village grabbed the yoke of the lead oxen and guided them along the path and up and over a small rise. David gasped as they reached the top. Spread before them was a valley filled with round huts. Each hut had a perfectly cone-shaped straw roof. David caught a glimpse of women and children peering around the edge of the doorways of the huts.

"They are telling us to get off the wagon," said Pomare as they rolled to an easy stop. "I think they want to introduce us to their chief."

David climbed down from the wagon and ran his fingers through his wiry brown hair. This was going to be a very big moment; he was about to be introduced to his first African chief.

"Wait here," instructed Pomare, interpreting the Bantu words of their hosts. A minute later David heard the loud, rhythmic beating of drums. He turned in the direction it was coming from and saw a large man dressed in a lion skin cloak. The mane of the skin was pulled around the man's neck, making the man look especially regal. The man was surrounded by warriors, each carrying a spear and a gray, rhinoceros skin shield.

"Greetings," said David to Pomare. "Tell him we bring greetings."

Pomare spoke in Bantu and then turned back to the missionaries. "Chief Moseealele says you are welcome. These are Bechuana people, and this village is called Mabotsa.

David smiled a broad smile. He wished he could speak Bantu, because then he would be able to understand everything that was being said. It frustrated him to think these people had so much information he could not discuss with them.

The exciting afternoon turned into an equally exciting evening. Chief Moseealele ordered a cow be killed for a feast, and as they ate and drank together, the missionaries watched the people dance and chant. David was captivated by all he saw, and that night by the light of his oil lamp, he tried to write down everything that had happened. As he blew out his lamp and lay down to sleep on the woven mat that had been provided for him, he thought he saw the dirt on the floor move. He shook his head and looked again. He told himself he must have imagined it as he pulled a blanket up over his shoulders.

The next morning David awoke and stretched his body. When he sat up, he stared at his fingers. Between each finger were dozens of tiny, dark blue balls not much bigger than pinpricks.

"What's this?" David asked Roger Edwards, who was still lying on his mat.

Roger shot straight out of bed as soon as he saw David's hands. "Tampan," he exclaimed. "I should have thought of this! Tampan are African lice, and they burrow beneath the skin in the night."

David went to scratch his hand.

"No, don't do that!" yelled Roger. "If you scratch, their heads will fall off inside, and then you'll have to dig them out with a needle."

"Then how do I get rid of them?" asked David. "They do come out, don't they?"

Roger grunted. "Yes," he said. "They come out, but not easily. First we'll have to douse them with alcohol and then burn them out with the end of a hot needle."

The next hour was spent laboriously removing the lice one by one. David learned from Roger Edwards that the lice live in the dirt.

"So that's why I thought I saw the floor moving last night. It was all the tampan lining up to jump on me!" David said. "But how do we stop them? Surely we can't do this every morning for the rest of our trip."

"No," replied Roger. "The problem is that we slept on a bare floor. The floors back at the mission house are all plastered over, so the lice can't live in

them. Tampan also don't like fire, as you can see."
He pulled a needle from the fire and very carefully
pressed it against one of the tampan on David's left
hand. The tampan sizzled with the heat, let off a
peculiar odor, and then dropped off. "If we have to
sleep on the ground, we need to scorch the area and
lay a tarpaulin down before we pitch our tent."

"But how can we do that? The chief made a big
show of giving us this hut to sleep in. Wouldn't it
insult him if we didn't use it?" inquired David.

The question hung in the air. The two men knew
that they were indeed blessed to have been welcomed into the village at all. The last thing they
needed was to insult the chief by refusing his hospi-
tality. However, as the day unfolded, so did an
answer to their dilemma.

"They want me to get things out of the wagon,"
said Pomare as the missionaries sat eating corn-
cakes for breakfast.

"What kind of things?" asked David.

"They don't know, they're just curious," replied
Pomare.

David smiled as he looked over to where the
wagon stood. Several groups of people had gathered
near it, poking at its wheels and canvas canopy.

"Well, let's see what we can do for them," said
David, scrambling to his feet.

An hour later, the entire village was in an uproar.
The people loved David's shaving mirror most of
all. They passed it from one person to the next, each
trying to make a funnier face in the mirror than the

person before. They laughed until tears ran down their faces.

"They want to know what is in that black bag," Pomare said to David.

"You'll have to tell them they can't touch the things in there. That's my medical bag. Do you think they know what a doctor is?" David asked.

"I'll try explaining it," said Pomare. "They have a witch doctor in the village, for sure."

The people did understand that the things David Livingstone had in his bag could cure them, and they immediately began to ask him for help.

It was then that David had his idea. "I would like to help you," he said, "and I will. But first you must let me put up my medicine tent. My medicine works best in there."

The people understood perfectly and waited patiently while David and Roger scorched the ground and then pitched their tent. For the rest of the day, David doctored the people, most of whom had infections of one kind or another that had not properly healed. As he worked, David asked Pomare to interpret for him so that he could learn as much as he possible about Bechuana people's customs and ways of looking at the world. One thing he learned was how the work was divided up in the village. The women did the gardening, built and maintained the huts, collected firewood, and cooked the meals. The men's job was to hunt for food and turn what they did not eat into things to wear. The men were expert at tanning skins and making them into clothes for everyone in the village. David was startled to learn that the people even had a way to make metal spearheads, though Pomare told him that the exact process was a closely guarded secret.

That night, the two missionaries slept in the "medicine tent." Much to his relief, David awoke the next morning free of tampans.

The men had more medical work to do the next day and the day after that, but finally on the fifth day, it was time to leave.

"Are we headed back to Kuruman?" asked Roger as they folded the tent and loaded it onto the wagon.

David looked at his partner. Even though Roger Edwards had been a missionary in Africa for many years, he already expected David to make all the decisions. This was a decision David was only too glad to make. "No. We have come so far, we might as well press on farther north before we turn back," he announced. Then seeing the panic in his partner's face, he added, "I don't think Reverend Moffat will beat us back."

Roger nodded glumly, and David felt a surge of frustration. *Why doesn't he want to go on? Are all missionaries so ready to scurry back to their own homes and forget the thousands, maybe millions of people out here who have never heard the gospel message?* David didn't have an answer. What he did know, despite his short time in Africa, was that he was different from other missionaries. The missionaries he had met so far were settlers; he was a pioneer, a trailblazer. He had a burning passion in his heart to push farther out into the unexplored areas. He didn't know where this desire would take him; all he knew was that God had given it to him, and somehow God would use it for good.

A Second Trip North

The wagon rumbled northward. Every hour David Livingstone would pull out his compass and take a reading. In a notebook he would record the exact direction they were headed and jot down a careful description of the land they were traveling through. Four days after leaving the village of Mabotsa, the group arrived at a village belonging to the Bakwains, a subtribe of the Bechuana people. Again the travelers were welcomed into the village, where the people poked and prodded at their belongings. Most of them had never seen a white person before, and they insisted David roll up his shirtsleeves so they could examine his skin more closely. They spat on his freckled forearms and rubbed vigorously, then laughed with surprise when his freckles would not rub off. They also peered at the two white missionaries' long bumpy noses, pinching them to make sure they were firmly attached to their faces. "Long noses," the children giggled as they danced around the men with glee.

Once again, the missionaries were offered a hut to sleep in by the chief, but this time David was ready. He explained that he was a doctor and needed to use his own tent to make medicine. Once the word was out that he could cure people, he was pressed to examine all manner of ailments from sore eyes to infected feet.

The visit with the Bakwains was a great success, and David began wondering why it was so hard to make friends with the tribes around the mission at Kuruman. One night as he and Roger Edwards lay in their tent, he asked about this. "Why is it that the people here are so much more friendly to missionaries?"

David heard Roger Edwards clear his throat. "Umm. I think there are a lot of reasons, but probably the main one is the whole problem of marriage. The way to show you are an important man in Africa is to have many wives. If you can support many wives and all the children they produce, it shows you have a lot of wealth."

"That makes sense," said David.

"Well, yes it does. But it's not God's way. The Bible teaches that each man must have only one wife, and that's where the problem begins. When a native man becomes a Christian, he has to give up all but one of his wives. The natives don't want to do this, and they end up despising missionaries and the gospel message."

"How do we get around that?" asked David.

"I don't see that we do," said Roger, rolling over on his cot. "It's a matter of getting to the children young, before they marry, I think. Once they have more than one wife, it's very difficult to get them to budge." He yawned loudly. "Well, I'm sleepy, how about you?"

"Yes, me too," replied David, although his mind was already racing. He lay on his back on his cot for a long time, thinking about the whole problem of converting Africans. He could see what a problem having many wives could be, but there had to be some way to reach the African men. There had to be some way around the problem, though right then he couldn't think what it might be.

The two missionaries stayed in the village for a week, and David made many friends as he treated their endless ailments and illnesses. When he announced it was time for him to return to Kuruman, the people of the village were upset.

"What have we done wrong to send the white men away?" they asked Pomare. Then they begged, "Please tell them to stay with us until the rainy season starts."

"Tell them I will be back," David instructed Pomare. "And the next time I come I will stay longer."

This seemed to cheer the people up a little, and they crowded around the wagon to say farewell to their new friends.

The trip back to Kuruman was slow. David insisted on taking a different route so that he could take notes and add details to his map along the way. The villages were small and sparsely spread along this route, and it was not until they were about one hundred fifty miles from Kuruman that they came across a village of any size. It, too, was a Bakwain village, and the men stopped to introduce themselves. However, Sechele, the village chief, sent word to them that he could not entertain them properly because of his sore eyes. David was able to supply him with some ointment that began to cure his problem. Chief Sechele and the missionaries then sat down together to a meal of milk and beans. The chief was so grateful for the ointment that he presented the missionaries with a deer carcass to take along for food on the remainder on their journey. David thanked him and promised to return to visit him on his next trip north.

As David and Roger Edwards left the village, they had no idea they were being followed. They had gone about ten miles when David pulled the wagon to a halt and they began to set up camp for the night. As they were preparing a patch of ground on which to pitch their tent, David heard an unfamiliar sound under the wagon. He stopped and listened. There it was again. It sounded almost like sobbing. When David crawled under the wagon to investigate, he found a girl who looked to be about eleven years old. The girl was naked except for many strands of colorful beads draped around her neck and body. Tears were streaming down her face.

"What are you doing here?" David asked softly, and then he remembered that she wouldn't understand a word he was saying. He backed out from under the wagon and went to fetch Pomare, who was hauling water from a nearby stream. He waited patiently for Pomare to tell him why this girl had followed them out into the wilderness and why she was now crying so hard under the wagon.

It didn't take long for the girl's story to come tumbling out. The girl's parents had died when she was very young, and her older sister had taken care of her since then. However, the week before, her older sister had died, too, and now an uncle had decided to sell her as a wife to someone in the village. The girl did not want to be married. Instead, she wanted to stay with some friends who lived near Kuruman. When she heard that that was where the missionaries were headed, she followed the wagon, waiting until she was far away from the village before showing herself.

Pomare had just finished relating the girl's story when a warrior with a gun slung across his shoulder came running down the trail towards them. David looked around frantically. He guessed the warrior had come to retrieve the girl, but it was too late to hide her. David stepped in front of the girl and waited. As soon as he got close, the warrior started yelling in Bantu. He had come for the girl, who had been promised to his brother as a wife.

David quietly prayed under his breath. He admired the girl's plucky determination, and he made it clear to Pomare that she would not be forced to return to the village. After several minutes of heated exchange between Pomare and the warrior, an agreement was worked out. If the girl returned all the beads she was wearing (which were used as money) she would be free to travel on with the missionaries. The girl quickly unwound the beads and handed them to the warrior, who seemed satisfied with the outcome of the situation as he trotted off back along the trail.

For the rest of the journey the girl traveled with the men. Sometimes she walked alongside the wagon with Pomare and the other African guide. At other times she rode in the wagon beside David, chattering away to him in Bantu the whole time.

Finally, in December 1841, the travelers arrived safely back in Kuruman. The girl was reunited with her friends, who welcomed her into their hut.

Roger Edwards seemed particularly relieved to find that the Reverend Moffat hadn't returned in their absence. In fact, the reverend had sent a letter saying that he would be staying in England even longer than planned. The printing of the New Testament in the Sechuana dialect was taking longer than expected, and the London Missionary Society had been so impressed by his talks on Africa that they had asked him to write a book about his missionary work before he returned. So the Reverend Moffat was hard at work writing a book, which he had decided to entitle *Missionary Labors and Scenes in Southern Africa.*

Upon his return, David was thrown straight back into the life of the mission station at Kuruman. Since he was the only doctor for hundreds of miles, people flocked to the station for help. And while David tried his best to treat all those who came to him with medical needs, he kept reminding himself that he had not come to Africa just to stay in one place and lance boils and bandage wounds. He had come to preach the gospel message to people who had never heard it before. And so, almost as soon as he arrived back at Kuruman from his trip north, David began planning another trip. This time, though, Roger Edwards made it clear he would not go along. For him, it was just too dangerous to take such a risk again. But not for David Livingstone. Indeed, by now his fellow missionaries had figured out that David actually seemed to thrive on taking risks.

In February 1842, David set out on a second trip north. This time he took four Africans with him, Pomare and the other guide from the first trip plus two men to take care of the wagon and tend to the oxen.

On this trip, David wanted to return to visit the Bakwains, particularly Chief Sechele, as he had promised, as well as map out some more of the countryside. He chose a different route from before to take him north, and although he did end up among the Bakwains, it was not the group he had anticipated. He arrived at another village, the residents of which, although they were Bakwains, were bitter enemies of Chief Sechele and his village. This village was called Lepelole, and it was led by a chief named Bubi. When Chief Sechele was a young boy, Chief Bubi had killed his father, and from that time on, hatred had erupted between the two villages.

David refused to take sides in their hostilities and instead spent his mornings treating the sick and injured and his afternoons working alongside and talking to the people of the village. By doing this, he was able to quickly pick up the Bantu language until he was able to speak it quite fluently. He did, however, make a few embarrassing mistakes. Since Bantu is a tonal language, the same word could have several meanings, depending upon the tone in which it was spoken. In the course of preaching about sin, David discovered that because of his pronunciation he was actually preaching against cow dung!

Regardless, David was given much respect in the village because of his ability to heal people. Only one other man in the village was given the same level of respect, and that was the rainmaker. Because the people of the village had no way to get a lot of water from the river to their crops, regular rain was very important to them. Hence, it was the rainmaker's job to make sure it rained regularly.

Thinking back to the irrigation system at Kuruman, David decided it was time to do something about the problem and in the process make the rainmaker obsolete. He laid out a string about four hundred fifty feet in length from the river to the gardening area. David wondered how he could dig a channel that long. He had only one spade head without a handle, and he knew the Africans used only sticks to dig with. He decided, however, to dig with what he had. He stripped off his shirt, found the spade head in the wagon, and began to dig. Soon a crowd of curious onlookers gathered around him. After watching for a while, one man picked up a stick and joined David. Others followed his lead until over one hundred people were scraping and picking at the dirt along the line of string. A system using tortoise shells and wooden bowls to scoop out the dirt and cart it away was soon developed.

After several days of hard work, the channel was finally finished and water flowed to the crops growing in the garden area. Everyone, including the village rainmaker, was pleased with the results. By the time David was ready to leave, he had become the most popular man in the village. Still, despite his popularity, he was determined to press on farther north. He said farewell to Chief Bubi, promising him they would meet again.

Soon after David left Lepelole, he received word that Chief Bubi had died. The chief had asked the village witch doctor to remove an evil spell he was convinced someone had put on him. The witch doctor had decided to do this by standing Chief Bubi next to a tree he intended to blow up with gunpowder. He felt sure the blast would frighten away the evil spirits that had brought the spell to the chief. Regrettably, the chief was standing too close to the tree and was killed by the explosion.

David was very discouraged when he heard what had happened. He had told Chief Bubi many times that God was the only one who was able to help him find the peace of mind he sought. Now it was too late. The chief had died a senseless death.

David stretched out the map of Africa in front of him. He had filled in many details on it from his travels, but as he examined the area directly north, he had no real clue as to what might lie ahead. All the map said of this area was "Unexplored Kalahari Desert." David refolded it and slipped it back into his leather satchel.

Everyone in the group was now walking. The wagon and all but four of the oxen had been left behind. The plain the men were about to cross was too sandy, and the wheels of the wagon would have become stuck in the sand almost immediately. The men had loaded their things onto the backs of the four oxen, which they now led. As he trudged on, David was thrilled to think that he was the first white person to see the scrubby hills and windswept valleys the group was walking through.

Even though the men were only on the southern edge of the Kalahari Desert, getting enough water each day was soon a concern. The African guides, however, knew which plants were moist enough to squeeze water from when they could find no springs.

After two weeks of trekking northward, the group arrived at a Bamangwato village, ruled over by Chief Sekomi. The three thousand or so people who lived in the village gave the travelers an enthusiastic welcome. David went straight to work treating the sick and learning as much about the villagers' culture as he could. Whenever the opportunity arose, he spoke to people about God's love for them, but it was difficult for the people to grasp the full meaning of what he said. The people had never heard of such a God before, and the very word *God* itself caused confusion. The Bamangwato word for God meant "a very important person or being," and so the people spoke of many gods. When David cured people of their medical problems, the people even called him God!

It was all very difficult, but David was determined to find some way to get the idea across to the people of the village. He knew he had succeeded to some extent when Chief Sekomi visited him in his tent one evening. After some brief talk about what had gone on during the day, Chief Sekomi came right to the point. He looked David in the eye and said, "I have come here to ask you for something. Give me some medicine that will change my heart. I am too proud, and I always feel angry with my people. I don't want to be like that anymore."

David reached for his Bible. "My friend," he said, holding it up, "the only medicine that will change your heart is found in this book, if you will...."

"No, no," interrupted the chief. "You don't understand. Now. I want my heart changed now. I want medicine that will change me now."

Of course, David had no medicine for Chief Sekomi's condition, and after a few more minutes of demanding the impossible, the chief left.

The next day the chief did not mention his visit of the night before, but David was encouraged to think that at least Chief Sekomi knew he needed something to change his heart. Now all David had to do was think of a way to explain exactly what it was the chief needed.

David was determined to go about twenty miles farther north to visit the Bakaa tribe, and he told Chief Sekomi of his plans. The chief's eyes opened wide. "No," he warned, "you must not go to the Bakaa. They are vicious people. They will surely kill you as they killed the other white man and his group."

David frowned. He had not heard about any other white people in the area.

"Who were they?" he asked.

"I do not know his name, but he was a trader traveling from the east." Chief Sekomi lowered his voice for dramatic effect before going on. "I hear they poisoned his food and water, and when all his party died, they killed his oxen and ate them."

"I will have to be extra careful then. Thank you for the warning," replied David.

"You would still go?" asked Chief Sekomi incredulously. "I do not understand you. You risk death for what?"

"To find out who lives there, and to prepare the way for the gospel message," said David firmly.

"Well," said Chief Sekomi, rubbing his chin. "If you must go to the Bakaa, you will not go alone. I will send four of my warriors with you, though I fear you will all perish."

David thanked the chief and returned to his tent to pack his belongings for the trip. He wondered whether the chief was right. Was it a suicide trip? Perhaps it would be safer to just turn around and head back to Kuruman, but David Livingstone had been stubborn all his life. He was the only weaver in Blantyre to become a doctor, and the only doctor in his class to become a missionary. When he made up his mind about something, he did it. And he had made up his mind. Despite the danger, he was going to find out who lay to the north, and that was all there was to it.

Chapter 9

Mabotsa

Run! Quickly, this way. We must hide."

The people of the village fled at the sight of David Livingstone and his men. By the time David was standing outside the largest hut, only three people were left in the entire village: the chief, with a scowl on his face, and two of his servants. The servants looked fearfully at David, and the chief spoke harshly to them. "Stay here. I will not flee my village like an antelope running from a lion." Then he walked up to David and looked him in the eye. "You are not welcome here. My people say you have come to avenge the death of the trader, but you would be a fool. Go now, while you can."

David stood his ground. His mind whirled as he thought about what the chief had said. The whole village was afraid of him. The villagers were afraid he had come to kill them because they had killed a white man. No wonder they had fled! Now David had to think of a way to convince them he had come in peace. But how?

In an instant, a plan flashed through David's mind. David had to show the villagers they had nothing to fear. Careful not to make any sudden moves, he pulled a sack of cornmeal from one of the bags slung on the back of an oxen. He poured some of the meal into a pan and asked the chief for some water to mix it into a mush. When the chief looked confused, David knew his plan was working. The trader had been given poisoned water, and now David was showing the chief he was not afraid he might get the same treatment. Finally, one of the chief's servants brought him an ostrich egg filled with clear water, which David stirred into the corn-meal to make the mush.

"Thank you," said David. "This will do just fine." Then he walked over to one of the fires that had been abandoned and heated the mush over it.

Keeping his eyes firmly on the chief, David eventually sat down cross-legged on the dusty ground and ate the mush right out of the pan. "Delicious," he said, making sure he ate every scrap. "I think it's time for a nap now," he continued, lying down beside the fire. "I hope we can talk as friends when I wake up."

"I told you you're not welcome here," bellowed the chief. "Get up and leave now."

David lay still and prayed silently as the chief stood over him, his spear in hand. The chief stood there for about two minutes before turning and walking away in disgust.

David was awakened half an hour later by an amazed Pomare. "It's all right. The others have come back, and they say we can stay in the village. They are preparing food for us!"

Sitting up, David brushed the dust from his sail-cloth pants. "Thank God," he said in English, smiling at Pomare. "They know they have nothing to fear in us, and since we trust in God, we have nothing to fear in them."

Soon the chief and some of his elders were sitting down with David and his party, eating and drinking heartily. About halfway through the meal, the chief looked confused and spoke to David. "You must tell me why you have come to my village. You do not wish revenge, and you do not have goods to trade. What is your reason for coming among us?"

David laughed. "You come to the point too quickly. When this feast is finished, I will talk to you all. I bring you good news."

After everyone had eaten his fill, David announced that it was time for the villagers to gather around. Spying a pile of rocks at the south edge of the village, he quickly climbed up on them. In Bantu, he shared the gospel message with the people of the village. The people listened carefully to what he had to say.

As David scrambled from his rocky perch when he had finished speaking, he fell and broke his finger. Although the pain was excruciating, he knew he could not let it show. To do so would make him appear like a child in the eyes of the people. African men and women rarely showed any outward sign of pain. David had observed this many times. He had even cut a one-inch tumor from a woman's calf muscle while she sat calmly talking to a friend about the corn crop.

David asked Pomare to help him set the finger in a splint. When his finger was properly bandaged, he continued to talk to people about the gospel message one-on-one.

David and the guides stayed in the Bakaa village for several days, and no one tried to harm them in any way. Indeed, the chief spent much time with David, talking to him and asking him questions. He also told David about the terrible fear the people of the Kalahari Desert lived in. To the north of them was a powerful leader, Chief Sebitoane of the Makalolo tribe, and to the east was the legendary Zulu chief, Mosilikatze. Everyone in the area feared an attack from one of these chiefs or the other. This was why everywhere David went, people begged him to stay longer. They thought it would make them safer having a white man living among them.

By the time David had to leave to return to Kuruman, he and the chief were good friends. In fact, the chief insisted his own son accompany David south to safer territory.

The chief's son turned out to be very helpful as the group made its way back across the edge of the desert. He knew about the various plants in the Kalahari that could thrive on very little water. David watched as the chief's son carefully dug up roots from the sandy ground and chose the fruit from specific plants to eat. As best he could, David drew each of the edible plants in his notebook, recording the parts of them that were useful or edible. Before the trip was over, he had identified thirty-two roots and forty-three fruits in the Kalahari Desert that could be eaten.

In late June 1842, David Livingstone arrived back at Kuruman; he had been away for nearly five months. Although the Reverend Moffat had not yet returned from England, Roger Edwards and William Ross had been working hard at the mission. Indeed, David was greatly impressed with their results. On July 13, 1842, he wrote to his father that "souls are gathered in continually, and sometimes from among those you would never have expected to see turning to the Lord. Twenty-four were added to the church last month and there are several inquiries...."

Although he was delighted by the success of his fellow missionaries at Kuruman, David couldn't get out of his mind the image of so many undiscovered tribes who had never heard the gospel message. Although he itched to head north again, it was not possible right then. Fighting had broken out among the tribes, and although David was willing to brave being among such hostilities, he could not convince anyone to go with him, at least not for a while. He was stuck in Kuruman for the time being.

Still, there was a lot to be done in Kuruman, and David set to work with enthusiasm. He visited the surrounding tribes and preached to them, mended the mission's printing press, supervised the building of a small chapel at another mission station, and visited the sick each afternoon. He was busy and happy, but always he had an ear open for news that the fighting had stopped and it was safe to travel north.

Eight months after completing his previous trip, circumstances were finally right for David and a group of Africans to travel north. First, David wanted to visit his old friend Chief Sechele and the Bakwain people. He knew the chief was angry with him for visiting and helping Chief Bubi and his village. Indeed, Chief Sechele had gone so far as to send word to Kuruman that if David dared to come back to the village he would not be welcome, and harm might even come to him. As usual, David was not put off by such threats, and after eight days of traveling, he arrived at Chief Sechele's village. It was not the same village he had visited earlier. That village had been destroyed by the fighting, and a new one, called Chonuane, had been built farther east.

Those traveling with David need not have been concerned about the reception they would receive from Chief Sechele. The chief was glad to see David again, and with good reason. The chief's son was very sick, and everyone expected him to die soon. A European doctor was his only hope. David immediately examined the sick boy. It did not take him long to make a diagnosis: The boy was suffering from severe dysentery. David gave him some medicine and watched over him carefully. Eventually, the boy began to recover. Chief Sechele was so grateful that he never mentioned the threats he had made against David. It was as if he and David had always been friends.

Chief Sechele began to ask David many questions about his religion. He wanted to know why, if it was so important for people to hear of this God, had it taken so long for white men to come and tell the Africans about Him. This was one question David had no answer for.

After visiting Chief Sechele, David pressed farther north and east, right into the territory of the Matebele people. Wherever he went, he was welcomed, and he spent many hours sitting at fires in the evenings listening to local stories and legends. Whenever possible he told his own stories about being a boy in Scotland, and always he was careful to include the gospel message with his stories.

Four hundred miles and four months later, David and his group rolled back into Kuruman. David hoped desperately that the Reverend Moffat was back. After all, David had been in Africa for two years now and was still awaiting instructions as to what he should be doing, but the Reverend Moffat was nowhere to be seen. There was some good news, however. A letter had arrived from the directors of the London Missionary Society giving David and Roger Edwards permission to set up a mission station farther north among the Bechuana people. David knew exactly where to build it. On his first trip north, he had eyed a piece of land near the village of Mabotsa where two streams ran together, creating a lush triangle of land covered with large, shady trees. That was where David and Roger hoped to establish the mission station.

Another letter was waiting for David when he arrived at Kuruman. It was from Mrs. Robert, the wife of a pastor in Scotland. Mrs. Robert had collected and sent to David twelve pounds to be used to hire a native Christian helper, or agent, as they were called, to be a preacher.

By the end of July 1843, David Livingstone and Roger Edwards were ready to head out and establish the new station. David used the twelve pounds that Mrs. Roberts had sent to him to hire one of the best native agents in the area, a man named Mebalwe, who was glad to go north with the group.

It was now winter in southern Africa, the best time of year for traveling. Before the group left, three hunters and their African helpers, who numbered about thirty, stopped at Kuruman. The three hunters, headed north on a hunting expedition, were Englishmen. Two had come to Africa from India, and one had come from the West Indies. Besides their African helpers, they had a number of horses with them that were laden down with tents

and all manner of supplies, from silver boot brushes
to folding water stands. David was repulsed by the
idea of hunting the wonderful African wildlife for
nothing more than a few trophies, such as a tusk or
a skin or a mounted head. Despite his feelings about
what the hunters were going to do, he greatly
enjoyed their company. He especially liked Captain
Thomas Steele, who was aide-de-camp to the governor of Madras in India. The two men struck up a
friendship and planned to travel north together.

This was the first time that David Livingstone
had been in the company of very wealthy men.
David chuckled to himself that money couldn't buy
much in the African bush. And for all the guides
and servants the three hunters had with them,
David was surprised that whenever they stopped
for the night, the missionaries always had their
camp set up long before the hunters and their
entourage. This was because the missionaries and
their African helpers worked as a team to set up
camp. David and Roger Edwards didn't just sit
around and wait for their helpers to set everything
up for them, as did the hunters. David wrote about
this in a letter home to his family.

> When we arrive at a spot where we
> intend to spend the night, all hands immedi-
> ately unyoke the oxen. Then one or two of
> the company collect wood; one of us strikes
> up a fire, another gets out the water-bucket
> and fills the kettle; a piece of meat is thrown
> on the fire, and if we have biscuits, we are at

our coffee in less than half an hour after arriving. Our friends, perhaps, sit or stand shivering at their fire for two or three hours before they get their things ready, and are glad occasionally for a cup of coffee from us.

Two weeks after the missionaries set out from Kuruman, they reached the site for their new mission station. They were welcomed by the Bechuana people, and after some negotiating, Chief Moseealele agreed to sell them the piece of land they sought for the mission station.

Roger Edwards got straight to work building a mission house similar to the one at Kuruman. The house was fifty feet long and eighteen feet wide, with a veranda running along one side of it. Within a week, the shell of the building was up, a feat that seemed to greatly please Roger. David, though, was less enthusiastic. Each day spent hammering and plastering was a day he was not spending getting to know the people. Still, since the building would serve as a good base for his missionary work, David helped Roger with the construction as best he could.

The work on the new mission house gave David time to think. After spending over two years in Africa, David was disappointed that his time there had turned out to be very different from the way he had imagined it would be. Getting things done in Africa was more often than not slow and complicated. Yet the African people themselves more than made up for these disappointments. David loved being with them, listening to them, learning from them, and, in return, meeting their physical and spiritual needs. Still, in a letter to a friend he outlined two specific problems that made a missionary's work particularly difficult, especially the job of taking the gospel message farther inland.

The first problem David outlined was fever. Various fevers and illnesses in Africa could kill a person overnight. Chief among them was malaria. Nobody really knew how people caught malaria, but if a white person stayed in Africa long enough, it was only a matter of time before he or she became seriously ill or died from it. So far David had not contracted the disease.

The second problem was the tsetse fly. There was no mystery here. This little fly was the scourge of Africa. It swarmed in many parts of the country, and its bite was fatal to horses, oxen, cattle and sheep. The animals would become weak and sickly and then flop down on their bellies and refuse to get up again. The tsetse fly made it risky to take any expedition inland using horses or oxen. At any time the livestock could die, leaving the travelers without any transportation except their own two feet.

There was a third problem, too, though David did not mention it in his letter, probably because it was not a problem in all parts of Africa. However, it was a very big problem around Mabotsa. The region was infested with lions. David had often wondered what would happen if he were ever to come face-to-face with a lion in the wild. He didn't have to wait long to find out.

Chapter 10

Tau, Tau!

It was midafternoon, and David stretched. He was sitting on the veranda of the new mission house with Mebalwe, the native agent. The more he talked and planned with Mebalwe, the more convinced he became that the way to reach Africans with the gospel message was by training up more people like Mebalwe. Mebalwe already spoke the language, knew the ways of the people, and was ready to give his life if necessary.

"On Thursday next week we will visit the tribes to the northeast," said David, thinking of all the opportunities that lay ahead of him. "I've discussed it with Reverend Moffat, and he thinks we should build an outstation somewhere up there in a month or so."

Mebalwe nodded. "It is a good thing the reverend is finally home," he said.

David could not have agreed more. Finally, in December 1843, they had received word that Robert and Mary Moffat and their three grown daughters, Mary, Ann, and Bessie, had landed at Port Elizabeth. David had been so excited that he had jumped onto a horse and raced off to meet the Moffats at the Vaal River, one hundred fifty miles south of Kuruman. At first David was a little embarrassed about his enthusiasm, but traveling back to Kuruman with the family had provided him with a good opportunity to sound out the Reverend Moffat about his ideas for developing new mission stations farther north.

Suddenly David's thoughts were interrupted. "Tau, tau," yelled a warrior standing right in front of the mission house. The warrior pointed towards the south.

"Lions?" asked David. "What happened?"

The warrior spoke wildly. "It's killing sheep on the hill. We must go now!" With that he ran off towards the cluster of huts farther down the path.

"Come on," said David grimly. "We'll have to get our guns and be the backup."

Mebalwe followed David into the house.

"I don't like to use guns in the village. It's a bad idea for the natives to rely on guns to get them out of trouble. It's a much better idea for them to use their traditional methods, but if the lion is killing sheep," David shrugged his shoulders, "what else can we do?"

A minute later David and Mebalwe emerged from the house. Each carried a muzzleloading rifle and a leather pouch filled with gunpowder and half-inch bullets. Outside a throng of men surged past the house armed with everything from spears to sticks and clubs.

"Let's go," said David, tightly grasping his rifle and stepping off the veranda into the crowd.

When they reached the hillside, a gruesome sight met their eyes. Nine sheep carcasses covered in blood were strewn over the ground. The rest of the flock were huddled together and bleating loudly.

"This is the worst attack I've seen," remarked Mebalwe, shaking his head. "But where is the lion now?"

It was a question everyone seemed to be trying to answer. Groups of men were cautiously poking their spears into the long grass and behind rocks.

"Over there!" came a sudden cry, and all eyes turned to a clump of grass beside a boaboa tree.

David peered at the clump. The grass moved, and David could make out the outline of the huge golden-brown body of the lion. He whistled under his breath. It was the biggest lion he had ever seen. It must have weighed at least four hundred pounds.

"Circle it," yelled one of the tribesmen. Obediently the men fanned out in a wide circle around the tree.

David and Mebalwe poured gunpowder into the barrels of their rifles, then placed a lead bullet in after it and rammed it down. They then hung back with their guns at the ready in case they were needed as the men of the village moved in on the lion. In a flash, the lion sprang towards the men, who scattered in terror. Before anyone realized what had happened, the lion was gone.

The men stood for a moment, too stunned to speak. Then they all began to yell at once. "Why had the lion gotten away?" they asked. "Why didn't they hold their ground and throw their spears?"

The men argued back and forth for several minutes, but they had no answers. David decided the men had simply lost their nerve at the wrong moment, and now the lion had escaped. It would be hidden back in the hills by now, and no one had the courage to go after it. Four men were left to stand guard over the remaining sheep while others picked up the dead carcasses and carried them back to the village.

Whatever had gone wrong, at least there would be roast mutton for dinner tonight, David thought as he turned to walk back to the mission house. "Come on, Mebalwe, let's head back. We aren't needed here," he said.

As the two men walked in silence along the path that led through some rocky outcrops, something moved in the undergrowth. The men stopped in their tracks. Suddenly David saw the flick of a tail—a lion's tail. The lion hadn't run away into the hills, after all. It was here, no more than ten feet away.

Without taking his eyes off the huge beast for one second, David reached over his shoulder for his rifle. He put the rifle stock to his shoulder, lined up the sights with the lion's eyes, and smoothly pulled the trigger. Boom! A flash of burning gunpowder erupted from the end of the barrel, and the lead bullet slammed into the lion's neck. The lion roared in agony, but instead of lying down, it crouched on its haunches and leapt forward.

Pain raced through David's body as the lion's jaws clamped down hard on David's left arm. The lion lifted David into the air and shook him like a cat shaking a mouse. Then David felt the beast's hot breath on his face and its saliva seeping through his jacket. The lion's claws rested on David's head, and David guessed that the lion was about to rip his skull open. Through the searing pain in his body he could feel his heart thumping wildly in his chest. In the background he could hear shouting, but he couldn't make out what was being said. It was just he and the lion, and the lion seemed to have the advantage. The lion shook David again, and this time David felt bones breaking and skin ripping.

Boom! Another gunshot rang out, and the lion dropped David like a sack of corn. David lay on the ground stunned for a second, and then he rolled over. "God, help us," he cried as he saw the lion bearing down on Mebalwe. The gun flew out of the African's hands as the lion closed its huge mouth around Mebalwe's thigh.

The men from the village who had been staring at the sight suddenly sprang into action. They hurled five, ten, fifteen spears at the lion. The lion made a final leap at yet another man, but the gunshots and the spears had taken their toll. As the lion fell dead, David slipped into unconsciousness.

Fifteen minutes later David regained consciousness. He was lying on the veranda of the mission house, with Roger Edwards bending over him. "Are you all right?" Roger asked anxiously.

David tried to sit up, but a searing pain shot up his arm and through his body. Then he remembered the cracking of bone he'd heard while the lion was shaking him. "You have to cut this jacket off me so I can see how my arm looks," he said. Then remembering Mebalwe, he grasped Roger's arm with his right hand. "What about Mebalwe? Is he alive?"

"Yes," replied Roger. "He has deep wounds from the teeth, but I don't think anything is broken."

David slumped back down onto the veranda. At least no one had died trying to save him.

"Bring me a knife," Roger said to his wife, who was hovering behind him.

Roger's wife was back in an instant with a small hunting knife. Roger held the cuff of David's jacket away from David's skin and began to cut. "It looks bad," he said in a low voice. "Lots of blood. What should I do?"

David tried to block out his pain and think of himself as he would any of his patients. "Is it still bleeding?" he asked.

Roger looked carefully at David's upper left arm. "No, it looks like it's stopped," he replied, counting eleven puncture marks from the lion's teeth.

"Then you'll need to feel along it. Start at the shoulder and work down. Gently." He braced himself for the pain.

"It's bumpy here," reported Roger.

Gingerly David moved his right hand to the spot Roger was holding. He ran his fingers along the bone. "It's broken, for sure—the humerus," he agreed. "You'll need to wash the blood off and then bandage it and splint it for me. Do you think you can do that?" he asked, noting the pale look on Roger's face.

"If you stay conscious and tell me what to do," Roger replied, obviously not relishing the task that lay ahead.

When his arm was finally set, David was left to sleep. The pain was excruciating, but he knew he was blessed. If the lion had dug its claws into his head, he would have been a dead man. Of course, being a doctor, David knew that there was the risk that his wound could become infected, and that could well kill him as easily as the lion's claws.

For many days, David lay on his back as his arm began to heal. He was grateful that his wound did not become infected. While he recuperated, he wrote many letters home, including one to his father. Since he didn't want to alarm his father, he wrote, "You need not be sorry for me, for long before this reaches you [my arm] will be quite as strong as ever it was. Gratitude is the only feeling we ought to have in remembering the event. Do not mention this to anyone. I do not like to be talked about."

As he lay on his back, David thought about the Moffat family—in particular, their oldest daughter, Mary. He had spent a lot of time talking with her as he accompanied the family on the last leg of their journey back to Kuruman. He had seen something in Mary, something that made him reconsider his original plan to stay single the rest of his life. He had always thought it would be too much to ask of a Scottish woman to give up everything to move to Africa. While he loved all of Africa's strange ways—from traveling hundreds of miles on an oxen or horse to eating unknown foods and facing snakes and other wild animals—he could not imagine any woman he knew in Scotland enjoying such challenges. What he had never considered was finding a European woman born and bred in Africa and familiar with all the continent's peculiar ways. Mary Moffat was such a woman, and the more he thought about her, the more convinced he became that she might be the woman to be his wife. David was impetuous and didn't want to wait around to find out how Mary felt about him. So, two months after the lion attack, when he was able to get up and walk around, he took decisive action.

"You're not saddling up that horse to ride it, are you?" asked Roger Edwards incredulously. "Your arm can't possibly have healed well enough for that."

"I'm tired of lying around all day. It's time I was up and about," David replied.

"Up and about, yes," said Roger. "But riding a horse! You're out of your mind!"

"Perhaps," agreed David. "But staring at four walls day after day is enough to make anyone crazy, don't you think? I'll be away for ten days or so. I'm going to pay Mary Moffat a call."

"Mary Moffat?" spluttered Roger Edwards. "At Kuruman?"

David smiled as he flung a saddlebag over the horse with his good arm. "That's right. Here, give me a leg up, would you?"

Roger was still shaking his head in disbelief as David, one hand on the reigns and the other hanging in a sling, rode off.

The trip to Kuruman was just what David needed. He was out and about again, and although he had been mauled by a lion, he wasn't afraid to be alone in the African bush. He believed that if he let the animals alone, they would let him alone, too, and mostly they did.

Back in Kuruman, after hearing about the episode with the lion, the Reverend Moffat wanted to know everything about Mabotsa. How was the church building coming along? How many children came to the school? Was Mebalwe working out well, and what was he doing?

After David had answered all the Reverend Moffat's questions, he excused himself to take a walk around the mission property. The mission was as beautiful as ever. The manmade canals flowed with spring water and fed smaller ditches that now watered over five hundred acres of garden plots. The plots were owned and cared for by local African families, and the Reverend Moffat gave the people advice on what to plant and when. Indeed, there was nothing the Reverend Moffat liked to do more than to get out in the garden himself, since he had been a master gardener before becoming a missionary.

David sat on a bench in the mission garden for a while. The scent of orange blossom and the chirping of crickets filled the air. As he sat, David thought about what he was going to do. While he had been recuperating in Mabotsa it had all seemed so simple. He would ride down to Kuruman and ask Mary Moffat to marry him. If she agreed, they would be married, and she would move back to Mabotsa with him. But now, as he looked around Kuruman, he wasn't so sure the plan was workable. He had forgotten just how settled everything at Kuruman was. The place ran like clockwork. There was not a weed in the garden or a blade of grass out of place.

Mary lived with her parents in a large stone house, where five servants did all the cooking, cleaning, and laundry for the family. Would she really want to leave all this and move to Mabotsa, where she would have to do her own cleaning and help with the cooking? And there would also be laundry to wash and floors to scrub. Not only that, David knew that he could not live the kind of life Mary's father lived. The Reverend Moffat liked to stay around the mission, tending the garden, talking with the local Africans, and working on his translation of the Bible into the local dialect. David thought these were all good things for the Reverend Moffat, but not for him. He needed to travel, map unexplored areas, talk with previously unknown chiefs, and preach the gospel message where it had never been heard before.

The longer he sat in the garden, the more David wondered about the kind of life he had to offer a wife. Would Mary Moffat be willing to accept such a life? There was only one way to find out. Clumsily he stumbled to his feet. By tonight, he promised himself, I'll know whether I'm going to have a wife or not.

Chapter 11

A Married Man

Dark-haired, twenty-three-year-old Mary Moffat tipped her head and stared at David Livingstone. "You are serious, aren't you?" she asked.

David looked into her deep brown eyes and nodded. "Yes," he said, "I would like you to be my wife, Mary. I know it will not be an easy life...."

"No life is easy," interrupted Mary matter-of-factly. "Look at my father and mother. Everyone thinks my father has the model mission station for all of Africa here at Kuruman, but no one knows how much work it takes to keep it all going."

David chuckled. He had picked a practical woman, that was for sure. "Well, what do you say, Mary?" he prodded nervously.

"Mary *Livingstone*. I like the sound of that!" she said, nodding her head. "Do you think January would give you time to build us a house?"

David smiled at his soon-to-be wife. "I think that will do just fine. A midsummer wedding, it is then!"

David could hardly wait to get back to Mabotsa and start building. Whenever a hunting party was traveling through on its way south, he would write a letter to Mary telling her how the house was coming along. He even drew pictures of the house for her.

The house progressed quickly. It was fifty-two feet long and twenty feet wide, a typical rectangular mission house. The front door led into the center room, which was the living room. To the left was a bedroom, and to the right a pantry and a study. The kitchen was a small building completely separate from the house. All kitchens were built this way because of the heat the ovens generated and because the ovens sometimes caught fire. If the ovens did catch fire, the fire might burn down the kitchen but not the entire house.

About halfway through the project, David ran into a problem, which he described in a letter to Mary: "A stone falling was stupidly, or rather instinctively, caught by me in its fall by the left hand and it nearly broke my arm over again. It swelled very much, and I fevered so much I was glad of a fire, although the weather was quite warm."

It took two weeks of complete rest before David was up and about again. David realized, however, that it was useless to try to lift his arm higher than his shoulder, so he gave up the idea of building a solid stone house. Instead, the house was completed with plastered mud walls. David used helpers from the village to do the work when his arm became too painful.

Roger Edwards could not help David because he'd had an accident in which he had crushed a finger. David doubted that Roger would have helped anyway. The relationship between the two missionaries had become strained, especially now that David was about to become Robert Moffat's son-in-law.

The two men disagreed over things small and large. Roger continually reminded David that he was the junior missionary at the station, both because he was thirteen years younger and because he had been in Africa only three years. However, David got on well with the Africans; he learned their languages quickly and was fascinated by their customs. He wanted the natives to have more say in the life of the mission and hoped to start a training program so that they could become preachers and teachers themselves. Roger Edwards was not in favor of this at all. Eventually, things came to a head when Roger showed David a stinging letter he had written to the London Missionary Society. David was shocked when he read it. Roger had written

about things David thought they had forgiven each
other for long ago.

Perhaps it was his Scottish sense of justice, but
something inside David Livingstone was stirred
when he read Roger's letter. David wrote an equally
scathing letter to the LMS telling his side of the
story. There was just one problem. David mailed his
letter off, unaware that Roger had had second
thoughts and had ripped up his letter instead of
sending it. Now, as David prepared for his wedding
in January, a blunt letter complaining about the
senior missionary in Mabotsa was on its way to
England.

The wedding was held in the church at
Kuruman on January 2, 1845. The Reverend Moffat
married David and Mary, and Mary's two younger
sisters, Ann and Bessie, were Mary's attendants.
David stayed on in Kuruman with Mary for two
months before the couple moved to Mabotsa.

Things in Mabotsa did not go well for the new-
lyweds. Roger Edwards and his wife had originally
left Kuruman partly to get away from the constant
direction of Robert Moffat and his family. They
resented Mary Livingstone's moving to Mabotsa.
They were not gracious and tried to make things as
difficult as possible for the young missionary's
wife. The letter David had written to the London
Missionary Society had caused a stir, and a letter
was sent to the Reverend Moffat asking him to look
into the situation. All in all, Roger Edwards and
David Livingstone had had enough of each other.

To David's way of thinking, Africa was a huge, uncharted land, and David was living in a tiny, remote spot with a man who irritated him every day. One of them would have to go!

David finally decided that he was the one who should leave. One evening after dinner, he decided it was time to tell Mary of his plan. "Mary," he began, as she mended a hole in his jacket, "I have something to tell you. I've been considering this for quite some time, and I think we should leave Mabotsa."

Mary looked up, startled. "But where will we go? Back to Kuruman?" she asked.

David shook his head. "Mary, there are already too many missionaries sitting around in the southern areas. I want to go somewhere where there are no missionaries. Somewhere where people have not really heard the gospel message yet."

"But the money," she replied. "And the baby."

David reached out and held her hand. "If God is leading us, we will have enough money, and you will be a good mother wherever you are."

Although David tried to sound confident, the same questions had been swirling around in his head. Mary was pregnant and due to have a baby on their first wedding anniversary, and the money *was* a problem. David had received seventy-five pounds a year as a single man, and the London Missionary Society had raised the amount to one hundred pounds when he and Mary married. Within a few months, though, there would be three mouths to feed on the extra twenty-five pounds a year. As well, starting a new mission station was costly. David knew this from his experience in setting up the Mabotsa station. Every spare penny he'd had went into the building and equipping of the mission station.

"Well," said Mary, breaking into his thoughts, "I suppose you have made up your mind, but I do hate to leave this house and all the work you have done."

"I do, too," replied David, looking around at the house, "but if I did it once, I can do it again. And my arm is stronger now."

"Do you have a plan?" his wife asked. "Somewhere in mind for us to go?"

"Yes," said David, his eyes lighting up. "I want to go farther north to Chonuane."

"Chonuane?" questioned Mary. "What makes you think Chonuane would be a good place for us?"

"I have been there before. Remember I told you about Chief Sechele. I healed his son, and we had long talks together. I think he might be key to opening the area up to the gospel message. He listens well and asks intelligent questions. I haven't found many people here who are as interested in Christianity as he is."

"Perhaps it would be a good idea," agreed Mary, "as long as we can be settled before the baby arrives."

The move forty miles north to Chonuane was completed just in time for the arrival of the Livingstones' first baby, who was named Robert, after David's grandfather.

Life at Chonuane was much more difficult than it had been at Mabotsa. Food was scarce, and a long drought had set in, making it impossible to grow the variety of fruits and vegetables that had grown in Mabotsa. Still, David was very happy at Chonuane, especially when he spent time with Chief Sechele. The chief had proven even more intelligent and eager to learn than David had first thought. David showed Chief Sechele a translation of the Old Testament in his own dialect—Sechuana— that Robert Moffat had prepared. The chief, who had never read a word in his life, was now eager to learn. Within two days, he could read and write the alphabet, and only six weeks later he was reading the Old Testament by himself!

David and Chief Sechele studied the Bible together every day. David also busied himself with building a house, doing medical work, and starting a church in the village. A year later, the Livingstones' second child was born. This time the baby was a girl, whom they named Agnes, after David's sister.

By now Chief Sechele had read the Bible through several times and had decided to become a Christian. David was thrilled about the chief's decision, except for one thing. Like every other chief in the area, Chief Sechele had more than one wife; in fact, he had five wives. Each wife was the daughter of one of his subchiefs, and the chief had married each of them to strengthen his ties within the tribe. Now, as a Christian, Chief Sechele was beginning to think that having more than one wife was wrong. David did not know what to tell him. Polygamy went against everything he had ever been taught was right, but Chief Sechele's wives depended on him, since each one had borne him children. David also understood that in African culture, divorce was a great insult to a wife and her entire family.

The two men talked at length about the problem, and in the end, David told Chief Sechele that he would have to do what he thought was best. The chief decided to go ahead and divorce his latest two wives as politely as possible. He gave them both new clothes and many of his possessions and sent them back to their families. There was an immediate uproar. Many people in the tribe questioned who Chief Sechele thought he was, taking on the white man's ways and forgetting the ways of his forefathers. But the chief would not back down. He was baptized, and although no one else in the village followed his example, he continued to live as a Christian.

David was deeply disappointed that the conversion of Chief Sechele did not lead to many more conversions. He wrote to the London Missionary Society, telling them of a comment one tribesman had made to him: "To be plain with you, we should like you much better if you traded with us and then went away without ever boring us with preaching that word of God of yours."

Chief Sechele thought he had an answer to David's problem. "Do you really think my people will eventually believe what you say just by talking to them?" he asked David. "I can only make them do something by beating them. Let me summon my head man, and with our rhinoceros hide whips we'll make the whole village believe!"

Of course, David could not agree to this forced conversion. He believed that in time, the people would understand that the God of the Bible was more powerful and more loving than any of their tribal gods. However, time was not on David's side. As the drought wore on, many people in the tribe wanted David to leave. Not only did the people believe that David had stirred up trouble with Chief Sechele, but they also believed that he had brought bad magic to them and had stopped the rain from coming.

Eventually, after two years at Chonuane, the drought drove David from the village. There was simply not enough water for a missionary family to live and grow a garden. In August 1847, David Livingstone, his wife, and their two children moved forty miles west to Kolobeng, a small settlement situated on the shores of a river.

Indeed, the drought had become so severe that Chief Sechele and the entire village at Chonuane moved with the Livingstones. At the new location, David immediately set to work building a mission house, damming the river, and planting crops. He was convinced that this time he had found the right spot to build another great missionary station like Kuruman. There was just one problem: the neighbors—not the other African tribes, but someone much more dangerous—the Boers.

Chapter 12

Where Others Have Not Planted

When David Livingstone first heard about the Boers, he had been impressed with their courage and determination. After all, over six thousand people—men, women, and children—had trekked northward from the coastal towns of Port Elizabeth and Cape Town into uncharted regions. In the process they founded the republics of Orange Free State, Natal, and Transvaal. Their exodus north from the coast, known as the Great Trek, began in 1835, six years before David arrived in southern Africa.

Now, though, these trekkers were David's neighbors, and David began to understand better who they were and why they had left the coast in the first place. It was very simple, really. The Boers were descended from Dutch colonists who had arrived in southern Africa from Holland in the seventeenth century and had established large farms for themselves. After they had enslaved the Hottentot tribes, who lived on the coast at the time, things generally went smoothly for the next one hundred fifty years. The Boers had everything they wanted—free labor, large tracts of land, and no one telling them what to do. But that all changed in 1814 when the Cape of Good Hope, the southernmost part of the African continent, fell into British hands. British law, including a ban on owning slaves, prevailed there. Through the efforts of William Wilberforce in England, slavery had been outlawed in all British territories. This meant that the Boers had to free their slaves and find some other way to work their land.

Understandably, the Boers were not happy at this turn of events. How dare the British tell them how they should run their lives, they protested. However, when the Boers realized the British were serious and they would be forced to give up their slaves, they decided to abandon their farms and move northward away from prying British eyes. So the Great Trek began. Within a few years, most Boers had abandoned the coastal areas and headed inland.

From the time David arrived in Cape Town and then in Port Elizabeth, he had not wanted to live around large groups of white people. He hated the constant arguing and bickering, and he wanted to live and work with native people far away from the influence of traders and slave owners. However, to the east of Kolobeng lay a settlement of Boers who had made the Great Trek, and these people were not happy to have David for a neighbor. They had already made slaves of six tribes in the area and now had their eyes on Chief Sechele and the Bakwains. It would be a simple enough matter for the Boers to round up this tribe, except for one thing—David Livingstone lived among them.

The Boers did everything they could to get David and his family to leave the area. They forbade David to preach the gospel message in their territory and told him that if he sent a native agent to preach in his place, they would kill the agent. David stood firm, however, and would not be intimidated into leaving.

Eventually the Boers got tired of waiting for David to leave and decided to attack the Bakwains at Kolobeng whether David was there or not. Their plan for the raid was simple, just like all of their other raids. They would force unarmed Africans from other tribes to go with them. When they reached the village they wanted to attack, they would push the unarmed natives to the front and use them as human shields. From behind the unarmed Africans the Boers would fire at the village. If the people in the village tried to fight back in any way, the unarmed Africans, not the Boers, would be killed. When the fighting was over, the Boers would take the women and children captive and plunder the village.

David heard a rumor about the Boers' intentions, and sure enough, soon afterwards a messenger arrived from the Boers commanding Chief Sechele to surrender rather than face the death or enslavement of his entire tribe. The Boers' actions enraged David, who climbed onto a horse and rode three hundred miles to Boer headquarters to protest what was about to happen.

When David arrived, he was met by several hundred men, saddled and ready to join the fight to enslave the Bakwains and take their land. Each man was armed with a rifle, while there were only five guns in the whole of Kolobeng. If the Boers were ever allowed to go through with their plan, a tremendous slaughter would take place in the village. David was appalled and went straight to their commander. After many angry exchanges and numerous threats, the commander finally agreed to call off the raid on Kolobeng. However, he refused to promise that there would be no attack on the area at some time in the future.

What changed the commander's mind was David's threat to write and tell people in England and Europe what the Boers were doing. David knew this would touch a raw nerve, since the reason the Boers wanted him out of the village was so that there would be no European witnesses to their actions. The Boers themselves were not proud of the tactics they used in battle and did not want people observing them and telling others about them. So David's threat to tell people in Europe what the Boers were up to changed the Boers' minds about attacking Kolobeng and won the day.

David was saddened by the whole situation. Africa might be vast, but the areas where native people could live without interference from the Boers was shrinking each year. As he thought about the situation, David decided he had to find a path north through the Kalahari Desert. If he found such a path, perhaps he could lead the Bakwains out of the reach of the Boers. However, mounting an expedition to search for a route north through the vast Kalahari was expensive. Since David had already borrowed against his yearly stipend from the London Missionary Society, he could not afford to buy oxen, horses, and supplies and hire the men he would need to accompany him. Still, he would not give up the idea. There had to be some way to finance such a trip. He would just have to find it.

David wrote to many people explaining his desire to travel north and search for a path across the Kalahari Desert. One of the people he wrote to was his old friend Captain Thomas Steele, one of the hunters who had traveled north with David and Roger Edwards on their trip from Kuruman to establish the mission station at Mabotsa. Although Captain Steele was too busy to make a trip into the Kalahari Desert, his friend Cotton Oswell had the time and interest to make such a trip. Cotton Oswell was a civil servant from India who loved to visit

Africa to hunt wild animals. He came from a very wealthy family and had plenty of money to spend on such pursuits. One day in December 1848, David received a letter from him.

"Mary, I don't believe it. Listen to this," he exclaimed as he read the letter.

Mary set her basket of laundry down and gave David her full attention. "What is it?" she asked.

"It's a letter from Cotton Oswell. He has landed at Port Elizabeth and is ready to mount an expedition into the Kalahari! He says, 'I have engaged ten servants, purchased two wagons, twenty horses and eighty oxen. As I write to you they are being loaded up with 300 lbs. of coffee, 400 lbs. of tea, 100 lbs. of salt, 400 lbs. of sugar, two cases of brandy, a box of soap, 10 lbs. of pepper, three bottles of mustard, and an assortment of buckets, silverware, dishes, and kettles. In addition to the food I have a telescope, a sextant, gunpowder, and cartridges.' He goes on to say, 'I would be honored if we could join forces on this venture.'" David looked up at his wife, his eyes shining with delight.

"God answers prayer!" Mary exclaimed. "Why, David, everything he lists in his letter must have cost him six hundred pounds at least to buy, and he's invited you along with him. How wonderful!"

Cotton Oswell also said in his letter that he would be passing through Kolobeng in March. Along the way he was going to collect his friend Mungo Murray, another hunter who would accompany them on the trip. This was the best news

David had heard in weeks, and he began immediately making preparations for Cotton Oswell's arrival.

David tried to convince Chief Sechele to go along with him, but with the threat of a Boer attack still hanging over the village, the chief felt he should stay home with his people. However, David did recruit thirty Bakwain warriors and guides to join him. He could not afford to pay them, but he promised to make room in his wagon for the tusks of any elephants they managed to hunt down. The ivory from the tusks was worth a lot of money in Port Elizabeth and Cape Town.

David had often heard the Bakwains talking about a great lake in the Kalahari Desert. The Bakwains called it Lake Ngami, and David had set his sights on finding it. He had learned the hard way that a mission station must be situated beside a steady supply of water, and Lake Ngami could be such a place.

Although he had never met Cotton Oswell, David was certain that any friend of Captain Steele's would be a good and honest man. Indeed, he had been so impressed with Thomas Steele that when Mary gave birth to their third child, he named the boy Thomas Steele Livingstone. Now David waited anxiously for Cotton Oswell and his party to arrive.

When the men finally arrived at Kolobeng, David soon discovered he had been right. He and Cotton Oswell liked each other from the moment they met. Cotton Oswell had no objection to looking for Lake Ngami, and he was delighted to find that David could speak some of the local dialects.

The expedition left Kolobeng on June 1, 1849. First it headed northwest to a village called Serotl, 120 miles from Kolobeng. Serotl was on the edge of the Kalahari Desert and was the last point marked on the map. It was a sobering moment for everyone as the group passed the last point known to white men. No one knew what lay beyond.

Passing Serotl, the expedition entered the territory of Chief Sekomi of the Bamangwato tribe. The chief *seemed* friendly enough and insisted that two of his men accompany the party to act as scouts to find water for the eighty oxen, twenty horses, and forty-five men who needed a large supply of water each day.

Before long, David began to suspect that the guides were actually leading them away from water. Although the Kalahari did not appear to have rivers or streams, there was water to be found if a person knew where to look. In places, the rainwater collected about five or six feet underground on top of "pans" of limestone. If a person dug very carefully in the right spot, he could find these pools of underground water. Since David had no idea where to dig for this water, the party wasted many hours each day digging furiously with spades and turtle shell scoops. Sometimes they found a little water, but it was never enough for all the people and animals. They whipped the oxen mercilessly to keep them moving, but no amount of whipping could induce the animals to walk for more than six hours a day over the burning hot desert.

The situation became desperate by the time they had been traveling for a month. They were 120 miles into the desert and too exhausted to turn back. They had to find a good supply of water—and fast. As David contemplated their desperate situation, something caught his eye. It was a small, naked figure running silently into the nearby bushes.

"Quick, over there!" David yelled to Cotton Oswell, who was riding a horse. "I think I saw someone over there."

Cotton Oswell turned his horse in the direction David was pointing and clicked his stirrups. Five minutes passed before he returned, walking his horse. A woman from a bushman tribe was trotting alongside him.

"Thank goodness you found someone!" David exclaimed. "I just wish we had some way to talk to her. I can't say a word in the dialect the bushmen speak. It's all clicks and popping noises. Very difficult, really," he muttered as he climbed into the back of the wagon. He emerged a moment later with a string of glass beads and a leg of cooked gemsbok, which he held out to the woman, who smiled and grabbed them.

"She understood that all right," grinned Cotton Oswell. "Now, if we can just get her to tell us where to find water."

The two men did a pantomime, scooping up imaginary water with their hands and drinking it slowly.

The woman smiled again and pointed to the north.

"I think she understands!" said Cotton Oswell. "Come on. Let's swing the wagons around and see if she will lead us."

David nodded. "It's our only hope," he said. Then he added glumly, "I hope she isn't tricking us like those Bamangwatos we had to send back."

The expedition followed the bushwoman on late into the afternoon.

"Keep your eyes on her. We don't want her to disappear on us!" David cautioned his Bakwain helpers. He need not have been concerned. Suddenly the oxen and horses became excited, kicking and lunging forward.

"Water," said Cotton Oswell. "They must smell water."

Sure enough, just ahead of them was a large spring surrounded by low bushes. While several men stood guard watching for lions, the oxen were unyoked and led down to the cool, clear water.

"It's wonderful," laughed David, splashing around in the water. When he turned to thank the bushwoman for leading them to the spring, the woman was gone. As he scoured the horizon for some sight of her, David thought he saw something—not the woman but something else. He squinted and looked harder into the distance. Could it be true, or was he seeing things? Far in the distance was a ribbon of shimmering water lined with large trees.

"Look over there," he called to Cotton Oswell. "Do you see anything?"

Cotton Oswell shaded his eyes against the setting sun and stared hard. His eyes widened with amazement, and his mouth dropped open. "A river! I see a river."

David nodded with relief and excitement. He had been worried it was just a mirage. The next day, July 4, 1849, however, the river was still there, lying tantalizingly in the distance. With plenty of water in their bellies, the oxen didn't take long to cross the distance to the river. By midafternoon, the members of the expedition were standing on the edge of the Zouga River—the most beautiful sight David had ever seen. Stretching to the north and south on either side of the river was a line of lush trees that shaded the sparkling clear water.

David took readings with his sextant and carefully recorded the spot on his map. He felt exhilarated. No white man knew about this river, and here he was standing at the edge of it. David felt sure that if they followed the river north, it would lead them to Lake Ngami. He was right. Twenty-seven days later and two hundred eighty miles farther north, the river broadened into a large, shallow lake. On August 1, 1849, two months to the day since he had left Kolobeng, David, along with Cotton Oswell and Mungo Murray, was standing on the banks of Lake Ngami. This was one of the greatest moments of his life.

David estimated the broad and shallow lake to be about seventy miles in circumference and no more than chest deep at its deepest point. The lake swarmed with all kinds of animal life. Large herds of elephants and buffalo trampled the vegetation on the shoreline, dainty antelopes darted about, and crocodiles bobbed their heads in and out of the still water. What seemed like a million different birds flew overhead or waded among the reeds at the water's edge. David was charmed by it all, but most of all he was inspired with thoughts of a mission station on the lake edge. He could hardly wait to get back to Kolobeng to write to the London Missionary Society to inform them of his wonderful find.

The trip back was much less taxing. The men retraced their steps, following the Zouga River south for three hundred miles and then heading off into the Kalahari. This time, though, they had David's map to guide them. On his map, David had marked all the spots where they had been able to find at least some water on the trip north, and once again they stopped at these spots.

Chief Sekomi was astonished to see the members of the expedition alive and well. He had been certain they would perish in the desert, and the two guides he had sent with them had tried their hardest to make sure that happened. But the men hadn't perished. They had made it all the way to Lake Ngami and back.

On the trip, Cotton Oswell had shot an enormous bull elephant with tusks weighing over one hundred pounds apiece. The Bakwains had killed some smaller elephants and collected the tusks to sell to ivory traders on the coast. Everyone returned from the trip happy.

David's family was glad to see David. It had been four months and nine days since David had left. Agnes, aged two and a half, was now chattering ceaselessly, and even baby Thomas dazzled his father by giving him a broad smile from his crib.

Upon his return to Kolobeng, David wrote letters to his family in Scotland and to Thomas Steele in India. He also wrote to Arthur Tidman at the London Missionary Society office in London. After describing his adventure, he ended the letter by saying, "I hope to be permitted to work as long as I live beyond other men's line of things, and plant the seed of the gospel where others have not planted."

In contrast to the success of the trip to discover Lake Ngami was a visit to Kolobeng by the Reverend John Freeman, a director of the London Missionary Society. The Reverend Freeman was visiting all the LMS missions in southern Africa. The last mission he visited was Kolobeng to see David Livingstone. The Reverend Freeman did not say much about what he saw there, but what he did say was depressing. He was surprised at how few converts David had to show for his eight years of missionary work, and he did not feel that the school was being run as well as it should be. The Reverend

Freeman thought that David had neglected his missionary work and told him as much. David tried to explain that it was not easy converting natives and that he thought that an important part of his work was finding a safe area for the Bakwains to live in as well as opening up new areas for missionaries to work in.

By the time the Reverend Freeman had left, David realized he had a serious decision to make. He had to admit he was not a very good stay-in-one-place missionary. His heart was in traveling, in spending a day or a week or a month with an unknown tribe, and beginning the process of helping them to understand the gospel message. The question was, How could he arrange things so that he could do this? Where would the money come from to do it? And, most important, what would his family do while he was away in unmapped and unexplored areas?

Chief Sebitoane

Now that David had settled in his mind that he was meant to be a pioneer missionary and not a settler, he itched to head north again into the Kalahari Desert. Chief Sechele had told him about a great chief, Sebitoane, who lived beyond the Zouga River. Chief Sechele was convinced that Chief Sebitoane would be key to opening the northern regions of the Kalahari to the gospel message. As a result, David was anxious to go in search of him.

"Mary, I must go north again and find Chief Sebitoane," David said at dinner one night.

Young Agnes looked forlornly at him. "But Papa, you were away all last winter, and you promised to help me in my little garden this time."

David glanced around the table at his wife and three children while Mary let out a deep sigh.

"How long will you be gone for?" asked Robert, his eyes shining with thoughts of adventure. "Can we come with you?"

Mary patted Robert's arm. "You know that's not possible, Robert. Your father has important work to do."

Mary then turned to David. "What are we going to do while you're away, and how long will you be gone?" she asked, tears dancing at the edges of her eyes.

David felt terrible. If only there were some way for the family to go along with him. Suddenly his mind started whirling. "Why couldn't you come?" he blurted.

Mary stared at him. "You can't be serious, not with me expecting another baby."

David laid down his knife. "But why not? If you need a doctor, I'm the only one from here to Port Elizabeth. And what if I leave you here? It's only a matter of time before the Boers attack. They have made their intentions plain enough. And think of it, Mary. If Chief Sebitoane were to ask me to stay and preach the gospel, you would be right there at my side. I wouldn't have to return here for you before I could do that." David took another bite of tough rhinoceros meat, amazed that he had not thought of this before.

"Do you mean it?" asked Robert. "We could really go with you on a wagon?"

"We only travel in the mornings and evenings, Mary," David added gently, sensing his wife's hesitation. "And if you or the children needed to camp for a day, we could do that, too. It will be so much easier than last time. I have maps of the area now. I know where to dig for the water holes. Besides, once we get to the Zouga River, we won't have a worry. There will be plenty of water. What do you think?"

Mary nodded slowly. "It does make a lot of sense. I am worried about how we would be protected while you're gone." She reached over to cut up Agnes's meat. "Let's think about it for a day or two and see what happens."

It took a week, but in the end Mary agreed that the family should go with David. Whatever happened, they would stick together.

The Livingstones left in high spirits early in July 1850. This time, Chief Sechele, Mebalwe, and twenty Bakwains journeyed with them. David made his wife as comfortable in the wagon as he could. Mary kept Thomas with her while David often took the older two children with him. Robert and Agnes loved to ride tucked together in front of their father on his horse.

Everything went much as David had expected, right up until the time his two oldest children became sick with malaria. By then, they had reached the Zouga River, but David had been unable to locate Chief Sebitoane or any members of his tribe, the Makalolo. David had been warned that there were many tsetse flies in the area he wanted to explore. Little was known about the tsetse fly except that its bite slowly killed cattle, horses, and dogs, and David could not risk losing his oxen. As disappointed as he was, he had no choice but to get his children home as quickly as possible so that he could nurse them back to health.

A letter was waiting for David when he returned to Kolobeng. He ripped the letter open and read. "Dear Sir, Allow us to convey our congratulations on your successful journey, in company with Messrs. Oswell and Murray, across the South African desert for the discovery of an interesting country, a fine river, and an extensive inland lake." The letter went on to inform David that he had been awarded the Royal Geographic Society's annual gold medal, along with a prize of twenty-five pounds for finding Lake Ngami.

David was astonished to think that anyone in England would be that interested in his exploration, but he was very pleased to have the money. He was already planning how to use it on another attempt to find Chief Sebitoane.

Robert and Agnes both recovered from their malaria, and a month after arriving back in Kolobeng, Mary gave birth to their newest baby, a little blue-eyed girl whom they named Elizabeth. Things did not go well, however. During the delivery, Mary suffered a mild stroke, which paralyzed one side of her face, causing the older children to become scared of her. And baby Elizabeth did not thrive. Within a month she caught a chest infection, for which there was no cure. David did what he could, but Elizabeth died two weeks later. After they had buried her, the Livingstone family went to Kuruman, where Mary's parents could help take care of the children while Mary recovered.

The following year, the family returned to Kolobeng, where David made plans for another trip north as soon as the wet season was over. David planned to take his family along with him this time, too, and his old friend Cotton Oswell would join them.

David's mother-in-law had some stern words for David when she heard what he was up to. No doubt her criticism was guided by the fact that Mary was pregnant again. "My dear Livingstone," she wrote. "To my dismay, I now get a letter in which [Mary] writes, 'I must again wend my way to the far interior, perhaps to be confined in the field.' O Livingstone, what do you mean? Was it not enough that you lost one lovely babe, and scarcely saved the others while the mother came home threatened with paralysis? And will you again expose her and them in those sickly regions, on an exploring expedition?"

David knew her letter echoed the thoughts of most missionaries in southern Africa. To them the northern region was no place for a woman and children. Despite what these other missionaries might think, David was determined to open up the region for future missionaries to work in. As well, Mary made it clear she would rather go north with him than stay with her family in Kuruman.

On April 24, 1851, David, with his family, set out on his third trip north into the Kalahari. Once again, Cotton Oswell had cheerfully borne the brunt of the expenses for the trip. He had turned out to be a true and loyal friend to David, and as he got to know the rest of the Livingstone family, he came to love and appreciate them all.

The trip went smoothly to begin with. Cotton Oswell and several of the guides rode ahead of the wagons on horseback. Using the map David had drawn on his previous trips, they located the "pans" of water and were able to dig down to them before the rest of the group arrived with the wagons to set up camp for the night.

The expedition made good time in reaching the Zouga River, where David learned from some of the local bushmen that Chief Sebitoane was camped along the Chobe River, across the great salt flats of Ntwetwe. The natives told David it would take three days to cross the flats, but they must go prepared, since there was no water and very little wildlife out there. David and Cotton Oswell estimated that they could carry enough water for three days in the wagons, as long as the oxen and horses were well fed and watered before beginning the trek. Neither man had ever taken a wagon across a salt flat before and did not realize how difficult it would be. By the third day, they were only halfway across. The wagonwheels kept breaking through the thin crust of salt, and the oxen had to be whipped constantly to make them keep pulling the partially stuck wagons.

David and Mary Livingstone began to panic at the slow progress. What would happen if they didn't find water soon? David confided in his journal that the possibility of the children's "perishing before our eyes was terrible." On the fifth day, they entered some grassland and were able to find a small water-hole. Some rhinoceroses had beaten them to it, and the water was black with their dung. But by now they were all too thirsty to care, and they knelt down and willingly lapped up the black water.

From then on they were able to find enough water to meet their needs each day, but with the water came mosquitoes that dive-bombed the children mercilessly, leaving huge welts all over their little bodies. Once again, David and Mary wondered whether they had done the right thing exposing the children to such dangers.

On June 18, 1851, two months after setting out from Kolobeng, they reached the Chobe River, where they found a native man waiting for them. The man, whose name was Tonuana, told David and Cotton Oswell that Chief Sebitoane had heard a rumor that some white men were looking for him and he had come more than four hundred miles to meet them. The chief was staying on an island thirty miles downstream, and Tonuana offered to escort the men to him.

It did not take David long to decide that the best thing to do was for him and Cotton to go alone with Tonuana while Mary and the others stayed with the wagons by the edge of the river. On June 21, David found himself being escorted downriver to be the first white person ever to meet Chief Sebitoane of the Makalolos.

As he paddled the canoe, David wondered whether he was being lured into a trap. What if Tonuana was leading them right into an ambush? Or what if right at that moment the Makalolos were preparing poisoned food for their guests? David muttered a silent prayer that God would watch over them.

The men paddled for four hours, with only the sounds of crocodiles slipping into and out of the water and waterfowl squawking overhead to break the silence. Finally, they came upon an island in the middle of the river, and David found himself face to face with fifteen naked warriors. The warriors ran into the water and eagerly pulled the canoe ashore. As David stepped from the canoe, the warriors parted and a tall, lean man wearing a leopard skin cloak walked towards him and Cotton Oswell. Without thinking, David thrust out his hand to shake the chief's. As the chief reached out to grasp it, David realized that he probably knew nothing of the white man's custom of shaking hands. Chief Sebitoane welcomed the men in Bantu and showed them into his camp. By now the sun was beginning to set over the trees.

Dinner that night was a huge celebration. The chief had ordered an ox be killed and cooked, and there was a lot of singing and storytelling. Throughout the festivities, Chief Sebitoane sat silently on a stool watching.

Later that evening, after the celebration had died down, David and Cotton Oswell lay sleeping beside the fire. Suddenly David awoke with the feeling that someone was standing over him. His heart beat fast as he scrambled to his feet. Standing in the flicker of the firelight was Chief Sebitoane himself. At the same moment, Cotton Oswell awoke.

"I have come to speak with you," said the chief.

"Please, sit down," said David, hoping Chief Sebitoane had come in peace.

After they sat down, the chief gathered his cloak around him and began to speak in a soft, low voice. He told them his life story from beginning to end. He described how he had outwitted other tribes and their chiefs and how his tribe had been driven north by the Zulus. He told of the cattle he had stolen, the rivers he had crossed, and the battles he had fought. The stories continued all night, with only the occasional interruption as David asked the chief to clarify something he had said. It was dawn before Chief Sebitoane finished his stories and got up and walked back to his hut.

By now, David and Cotton Oswell were very tired, but they were also thrilled with the way Chief Sebitoane had welcomed them and taken them into his confidence. David was particularly struck by the chief's intelligence, and he hoped that before too long the chief might become a Christian convert like Chief Sechele.

After five days on the island, Chief Sebitoane asked the men to take him back to their wagons so that he could meet David's wife and children.

Nothing could have pleased David more. The chief's men paddled them upstream. Much to David's relief, everything was well with his family. Chief Sebitoane was fascinated with the Livingstone children, the first white children he had ever laid eyes on. He stayed with them for a week before David and Cotton Oswell accompanied him back downriver to his camp.

It was then that disaster struck. On July 6, 1851, Chief Sebitoane fell ill with pneumonia. David visited him, but there was little he could do. Any treatment he tried might not work, and David knew that if he touched his new friend and the chief then died, he himself could be accused of killing him. Three days later, Chief Sebitoane did die. David was disheartened. He had many questions but few answers. It seemed so unfair that he'd had so little time with the chief. He had hoped the two of them could develop a long and lasting friendship.

David had another serious question to think about. The Makalolos did not know what to do with the white people who were now in their midst. Their new chief was Sebitoane's daughter, Mamochisane. What would she think of the white strangers? Mamochisane lived some distance to the north, and it would take a week to get a message to her that her father was dead and another week to get a reply from her about what to do with the white people.

David, Cotton Oswell, and the rest of their party had no choice but to wait for a reply, all the time praying that God would grant them favor with the new chief. Finally, after camping on the bank of the Chobe River for nearly a month, news arrived, and it was good. Mamochisane instructed her tribe to treat the visitors exactly as Chief Sebitoane would have and to help them go wherever they wanted.

It was wonderful news to David. He had heard that there was a large river about three days' travel away, and he was eager to be guided to it. In the end, he and Cotton Oswell left Mary and the children and the guides with the wagons and went ahead on horseback. The Makalolos had warned them that there were many small rivers and a large marsh to cross before they got to the big river. A man on horseback or on foot could make it across, but not wagons pulled by oxen.

It was not an easy journey, even on horseback. The tall swamp grass sometimes reached to their shoulders, and the men had to urge the horses on through crocodile-infested waters. On August 4, everything they had endured was made worthwhile in a single moment. David Livingstone and Cotton Oswell sat on their horses and looked down at the mighty Zambezi River, a huge expanse of water about four hundred yards wide, and deep, though how deep they could not tell.

David and Cotton's guide told the men about a huge waterfall on the river and offered to take them there. He said it was called Mosioatunya, "the smoke that thunders." As much as they wanted to go and see the waterfall right there and then, David and Cotton had to get back to the wagons because

Mary Livingstone was expecting another baby any day, and Cotton was long overdue in England. They needed to get back to Kolobeng as quickly as possible. The waterfall would have to wait for another day.

Chapter 14

Wherever He Laid His Head

It was September 15, 1852, a hot, sunny day like all the other days so far on the journey home to Kolobeng. The wagons were stopped beside the Zouga River. As the remaining scrawny oxen that had not died from the bite of the tsetse fly drank loudly from the river, another sound suddenly filled the air—the crying of a newborn baby. The baby was David and Mary Livingstone's fifth child, another son. David climbed from the wagon carrying the tiny infant in his arms. He first looked over at the river whose water had saved his life on an earlier trip and then looked down at the baby. "I'll call you Zouga," he whispered gently to the infant, "Zouga Livingstone."

And Zouga it was. Although the boy was officially named William Oswell Livingstone, the nickname "Zouga" stuck with him for the rest of his life.

Mary recovered quickly from the birth, but within a few days, Thomas came down with malaria. David fought to save his son's life, dosing him with quinine and keeping his body wrapped tightly in a damp sheet to quell the fever. He also drove the wagons up into some distant hills where it was a little cooler. Thomas lay sick for a month before finally showing signs of recovery. When he was up and about again, the party continued on the journey south.

The whole episode with the birth of Zouga and Thomas's near-fatal illness frightened David. For the first time, he wondered whether Mary's mother had been right. Was it selfish and stubborn of him to take his family along on the expeditions? The entire matter weighed heavy on his mind, and he spent long hours on the trip back discussing with Cotton Oswell what he should do. By the time he reached Kolobeng, he had made up his mind. Mary and the children should go back to Scotland, where they would be safe. David's family would help look after the children, who could all go to a proper school. As soon as he was sure of his decision, David wrote to the London Missionary Society asking them to help Mary with expenses when she returned home.

Despite her parents being Scottish, Scotland wasn't home to Mary Livingstone. Mary had been born and raised in southern Africa. The one time her parents had taken her "home" on furlough, Mary had found Scotland to be a strange and terrifying place. She begged David to allow her to stay with him. She would much rather risk a lion attack in Africa than attend a ladies' tea party in Edinburgh! But David was firm; he had made up his mind. He planned to go farther inland on his next expedition, and he would not risk taking his wife and children with him.

It was a dejected family that made its way south from Kolobeng to Port Elizabeth. David assured Mary he would join her in Scotland in two years and that his family in Scotland would love the children. Mary, though, wasn't so sure.

When the group reached Port Elizabeth, Cotton Oswell once again proved himself to be a generous friend. He gave Mary Livingstone a purse containing one hundred seventy pounds—it was well over a year's salary for the family. Mary was very grateful. Cotton Oswell also insisted on outfitting the entire family in new clothes. As David looked at what they were wearing, he was thankful for the generous gesture. The whole family were wearing the same clothes they'd taken with them on the expedition north, though the clothes were now patched and stained.

David watched as his family stood on the deck of the *Trafalgar* on April 23, 1853. He could see six-and-a-half-year-old Robert grinning from ear to ear as he peered over the railing. David smiled. He

could see that, even at such a young age, Robert
had his sense of adventure and drive to travel and
explore. Five-year-old Agnes stood holding tightly
to Thomas's hand while Mary stood grim-faced,
holding baby Zouga in her arms. David waved as
the mooring lines holding the ship to the dock were
let go. The *Trafalgar* drifted out into the bay and
hoisted its sails. When the ship was just a speck on
the horizon, David finally turned and walked back
to the boarding house where he was staying.

David remained in Port Elizabeth for three
months before again setting out for Kolobeng. He
was glad to be on his way north, not only because
looking at the ships coming and going from
England made him miss his wife and children all
the more, but also because the Boers in town were
very unfriendly to him. The Boers did not like any
of the missionaries from the London Missionary
Society because the missionaries often took sides
with the Africans in disputes. David was doubly
despised because he was also trying to open up
northern areas for the British.

David did not know, however, just how much
the Boers hated him until he reached Kuruman,
where he was delayed for two weeks while a broken wagon wheel was mended. On the day before
David was due to head back to his home in
Kolobeng, Masebele, Chief Sechele's wife, came
running into the courtyard of the main mission
house at Kuruman.

"Is Mr. David here?" Masebele yelled between
deep gasps for air.

David was inside the house writing in his journal. He looked up and frowned when he heard the voice, which he immediately recognized. But what was Masebele doing all these miles from her home? Something must be wrong. He flung his journal onto the bed and ran outside. "Masebele, Masebele, I am here. What is it?"

Masebele swung around to face David, who could see the terror in her eyes. She pulled a letter from the leather pouch that was draped around her waist and handed it to David. "Here. My husband wrote this, but he could not come to you. They are still hunting for him. It was terrible, so terrible."

In an instant David knew what had happened. "It was the Boers, wasn't it?" he questioned. "The Boers invaded the village, didn't they?"

Masebele nodded and let out a loud sob. "Two of my sons were carried away. About sixty of the people were shot and killed. The cattle and oxen are all gone, and they burned all of our crops in the fields. Mr. David, what are we to do?"

David didn't answer her. He tore open the letter and began to read. In the letter Chief Sechele filled in all the details. On September 27, six hundred Boers on horseback plus several hundred more natives had surrounded the village. They had wagons with cannons mounted on them and thousands of rounds of ammunition. The outcome was assured before the first shot was fired. The Boers had taken hundreds of slaves just as Masebele had said, and had killed sixty people. Chief Sechele and Mebalwe, David's African agent, had escaped, but they had nothing to go back to—no home, no crops, and no neighbors.

There was more bad news. The Boers had taken special delight in ransacking David's belongings, taking what they wanted and burning the rest.

David stood staring at the letter, trying to take it all in. His books, his medicines, his surgical instruments were all gone. Except for what he had taken with him, including his navigational equipment, a few books, and some clothing, he had nothing left.

Although it took David days to recover from the shock of what had happened to his friends and to his own home, he did come to see some good in it. Perhaps now every native in Africa would know he was not secretly on the side of the Boers. He also realized how close he had come to being caught up in the raid himself. If his wagon wheel had not broken on the trip, he would have been back in Kolobeng when the shooting started. It was unlikely the Boers would have let him live to tell about it. And what if his wife and children had been there? David couldn't bring himself to think about that.

David truly understood for the first time just how much the Boers hated him, and he decided not to make himself an easy target for them again. As well, his missionary goals were to open up the interior to the north and preach the gospel message wherever he went. He began to see that these goals could be accomplished without the need for a home base. From then on, David decided his home would be wherever he laid his head for the night. He would not maintain a mission station again.

Giving up ideas of a permanent mission station freed David tremendously. David could go where he wanted and stay as long as he chose. The first place he headed for was Linyanti in Makalolo territory where Chief Sechele had apparently escaped to. On the way to Linyanti, David met Chief Sechele, headed south on his way to personally protest to the English chief, Queen Victoria herself, what had happened to his people. In the following months, the chief made the thousand-mile trek to Cape Town. However, the chief did not have enough money for passage on a ship to England and eventually had to give up his quest and walk the thousand miles back.

In the meantime, David kept heading north and finally reached Linyanti, the main village of the Makalolo people. The people were glad to see him, especially since the great Chief Matabele was at war with them and Arab slave traders were making more and more raids into their lands. The world was changing quickly for the Makalolo, who hoped that David Livingstone would help them stay safe and make sense of all the changes.

David was introduced to Sekeletu, the new chief. Although Sekeletu was only eighteen years old, his mother, Mamochisane, had handed control of the Makalolo tribe to him because she did not care for the job herself.

David had been at Linyanti only a week when he came down with malaria. This was the first time he had contracted the disease. Although no one at that time understood that mosquitoes spread the disease, David did notice that there appeared to be some connection between them and malaria. He wrote in his journal that the mosquitoes were "showing, as they always do, the presence of malaria."

The malaria convinced David he needed to press on in his travels and find a better area that he could recommend to white people to settle. With the Boers to the east, the Portuguese and ferocious Zulus to the north, and the Kalahari Desert to the south, David decided to head in a northwesterly direction towards the coast.

On November 11, 1853, David set out from Linyanti accompanied by twenty-seven Makalolo guides and helpers and several oxen. Onto the backs of the oxen were loaded some elephant tusks and a few strings of beads for trading along the way, as well as David's navigational equipment, books, and clothes, the medicines the Reverend Moffat had given David, a lantern, rifles, ammunition, and a small tent. With these few belongings, David Livingstone was about to attempt a feat successfully completed only twice before in known history. He was about to cross West Africa, using canoes to navigate rivers where possible and completing the rest of the journey on foot. He had little of value to trade with the unknown tribes he would encounter along the way, and even less food. To supplement their food supply, the travelers would eat seeds, meal, and manioc roots that they could find along the way. And since David was the only one who could shoot straight, it fell to him to shoot the wild game they would eat.

David had not counted on its raining as much as it did. The ground soon became sodden and difficult to walk over. Everything made of metal, including his guns, rusted, and the leather on his boots mildewed overnight. Even his tent rotted and ripped. But these difficulties paled when compared to David's difficulties with the tribes whose territory the expedition passed through. The tribes nearest the Makalolos were friendly enough, but as the men moved farther westward, they met new tribes outside the Makalolos' sphere of influence who were not so friendly.

David and his men experienced several near heart-stopping moments when they were surrounded and escorted into villages to "meet" the chief. On these occasions David had to talk fast to avoid physical harm, but eventually he and his men were always allowed to go on their way. That is, until David came to cross the Quango River and ended up being taken to see the chief of the Bashinje tribe.

"No, you cannot cross the river," the chief told David. "Not until you give me something I want."

"What would that be?" inquired David wearily.

"A man or an ox or a gun would do fine," replied the chief, smiling to reveal his missing front teeth.

"That is outrageous, but we have some beads," said David.

"Beads! You would insult me with beads?" spat the chief. "I do not think you are in any position to be telling me what I want. In fact, maybe I need a man *and* an ox *and* a gun. Ha! You don't understand that I am the man of power here."

David tried not to change the expression on his face. He understood things all too well. The chief of the Bashinje could take everything from them, even kill them if he wanted. And if they did, no one would ever know. David began to pray silently. He could not afford to lose a rifle, even a rusty one, the oxen were useful, and he would certainly never hand over a hired man to become a slave.

"I need to talk with my men," replied David, desperately stalling for time.

"Very well," said the chief. "We will speak again in the morning. I do not think you will be going anywhere. You cannot cross the river without our help, and if you turn back, we will follow you." He let out a loud laugh.

David was far from laughing when he returned to his men to tell them the grim news. The men were all sitting around a small fire discussing what they should do, when they heard a rustle in the bushes behind them. David grabbed his gun as everyone's eyes turned towards the noise. Suddenly a man dressed in the uniform of a Portuguese soldier stepped into the clearing.

"My name is Sergeant Cypriano di Abreu, at your service," he said, bowing to David. "Is there anything I can help you with?"

For a moment David was too amazed to speak, but he quickly regained his composure and told the sergeant about their predicament. Sergeant di Abreu told them there was a Portuguese settlement across the river and he would ferry them there if they liked. In the middle of the night, the party left the riverbank. The Bashinje chief heard the commotion and directed his warriors to fire on them. Thankfully, the warriors were poor shots, and no one was hit.

Much to David's surprise, the Portuguese were very kind to him and his men. Sergeant di Abreu served them the best meal David had eaten since leaving Kuruman four and a half months before. He also gave David and his men enough rations to make it to the Portuguese trading post of Cassange, where he told David to ask for Captain Neves.

Captain Neves turned out to be as kind and helpful as Sergeant di Abreu. He gave David a set of his own clothes to replace the rags he was wearing and insisted on feeding the entire group. When the group was rested and ready to travel on, Captain Neves sent a corporal with them. The corporal had an official letter giving him permission to requisition whatever food and supplies he needed for David's expedition.

The corporal guided the group all the way to the coast. As they got closer, however, the Makalolo guides began to get nervous and whispered among themselves. They were going to see the ocean, but big ships traveled across the ocean, big ships filled with slaves. Eventually they became so anxious that they confided in David. Although he was unsure of exactly what would happen when they got to the coast, David promised the men he would defend them with his own life. He would never let them be taken prisoner while he was alive and able to prevent it.

On May 31, 1854, the expedition wound its way wearily into the port town of Loanda. By this time, David was so sick from a relapse of his malaria that he was forced to travel on the back of an ox. And even then, the group had to stop every ten minutes to let him rest. Still, David was strong enough to look up and see the Atlantic Ocean. He had done it. He had made the two-thousand-mile journey from Kuruman through the Kalahari Desert and West African jungle all the way to the west coast.

Before long, David found himself in front of the British consulate, an imposing brick building with a brightly colored flower garden in front of it. He swung open the gate, not knowing for sure what awaited him. He need not have worried. Mr. Gabriel, the consul, was amazed but glad to meet him. On seeing how sick David was, he ordered him straight to bed. The story of his adventure could wait until he was rested.

A week later a British warship birthed at Loanda. One of the ship's doctors called on David and was appalled by the missionary's physical condition. David was little more than a skeleton. The doctor ordered him to stay in bed for at least a month to regain his full strength and recover from the malaria and from dysentery. As he lay in bed, David corrected his journals and wrote reports home to the Royal Geographic Society and the London Missionary Society. At one stage, a British captain visited him and offered him free passage back to England on his ship the *Forerunner.* Although David refused the offer, he was relieved when the captain agreed to transport his letters, reports, and maps back to England. He knew that the London Missionary Society and the Royal Geographic Society would be glad to hear of his findings and that his wife would be glad to learn he was still alive!

If David had been on his own, he would have eagerly accepted the offer to return to England and deliver the reports in person. But he wasn't alone. He had brought twenty-seven Makalolo men with him to Loanda and had promised to return them home safely. So while a voyage to England may have been appealing, David knew what he had to do. He had made a promise, and he would keep it. Somehow he would have to get well enough to guide the Makalolo men home.

Chapter 15

An Easier Route
to the Ocean

David Livingstone was a man who kept his word, though it was four months before he was well enough to begin the trek back to Linyanti with his Makalolo helpers. The trip back was not so fast: The trip to the coast had taken nearly seven months; the trip back took one year. Along the way, David and his men faced many challenges. They arrived at Christmastime at Pungo Andongo, one hundred sixty miles inland from the coast, where David learned of the tragic fate of the *Forerunner*. The ship on which David had sent his reports and maps back to England had been wrecked on some rocks and all hands were lost at sea. David prayed a prayer of thanks that he had not taken up the captain's offer to sail aboard her. However, since all of his papers were lost, he had to set to work rewriting his reports and letters to his family and friends and redrawing his maps. This held the men up in Pungo Andongo for several weeks.

The expedition also had to endure the entire wet season while traveling. Often the men waded through thigh-deep water for days on end, and it was nearly impossible for them to find a dry spot to sleep. The best they could do was to find a high patch of ground and build up a pile of dirt and mud, lay grass on top of it, and hope that the "little island" didn't get swamped in the night or attract the curiosity of crocodiles.

At last, after twelve months, David Livingstone led his Makalolo helpers home to Linyanti. Chief Sekeletu and the entire tribe were astonished to see them.

"It has been so long. I thought you had all been lost!" exclaimed the chief. "How many of you have come back to us?"

"All of us," replied one of David's helpers. "Not one of us was lost."

The chief was speechless. Indeed, it was an amazing feat for twenty-eight men to walk more than two thousand miles through enemy territory, facing countless wild animals, sickness, and harsh weather conditions, without a single fatality or defection.

A week of dancing, singing, and storytelling followed the men's arrival back at Linyanti. Chief Sekeletu, dressed grandly in the colonel's uniform the governor of Loanda had sent back to him with the men, presided over the proceedings. Each of the twenty-seven Makalolo men who had made the trip told his story to the village. Never in the history of the tribe had there been so many stories to tell at once!

David was humbled to discover that the Makalolos had taken good care of his things while he was gone. The tribespeople had made a shelter for his wagon, and not a single thing had been touched or stolen from the belongings he'd left behind.

Most men would have wanted to rest after such an arduous journey, but not David Livingstone. He didn't have time to rest. He had a new mission to undertake. Arab traders at Loanda had told him there was an easier route to the ocean. The Zambezi River and its tributaries, if he followed them, would lead him to the east coast of Africa and the Indian Ocean. David needed to explore this route.

A month after arriving back at Linyanti, David was ready to go again. This time Chief Sekeletu trusted him with one hundred of his men and plenty of goods that could be used as gifts and to barter for food along the way. There were also twelve oxen and enough beads to buy a canoe. By November 13, 1855, they were following the Zambezi River. David and about forty men traveled in canoes while the rest of the men herded the oxen along the riverbank. Progress was slow but steady.

Before long, David heard the men beginning to talk about the smoke that thunders. He had heard the same talk from his guide on his first visit to see the mighty river, and he knew they were talking about the waterfall. This time he urged the men to show him this legendary place.

The group was still six miles from the falls when David saw enormous columns of white vapor billowing into the air. David could hear the faint sound of rushing water. The whisper soon turned into a roar as the canoe was swept closer to the edge of the falls. The paddlers skillfully turned the canoe and headed for an island in the middle of the river that overhung the edge of the waterfall. David dared not move a muscle. He knew that one wrong move could throw the canoe off course and send it careening over the edge.

The canoe landed safely on the island, and David climbed out. By now the noise was so thunderous that the men could communicate only by using gestures. The men pushed through the undergrowth to the far end of the island, where David lay flat on his stomach and wiggled his way to the edge. Below him lay the most stunning sight he had ever seen. Sheets of water, two thousand yards wide, rolled over the edge of the falls and tumbled three hundred feet straight down. The thunderous noise vibrated through David's body, and the vapor billowed all around him. David lay there for a long time taking in the incredible sight, and knowing he was the first white man to see the falls.

Finally, David knew he had to pull himself away from the scene. As he wiggled back from the edge of the falls, he felt he had to do something special to mark the spot. He pulled out his pocketknife and found a large tree. Carefully he carved his initials, D. L., and the year, 1855, into the trunk. Then he gathered some wild flowering plants and made a little native garden around the base of the tree. Stepping back, David smiled, pleased with his work.

Later that evening David struggled to put into words what he had seen. He wrote, "Pieces of water leap off it in the form of comets with tails streaming behind, till the whole snowy sheet become[s] myriads of rushing, leaping, aqueous comets." As he took his navigational readings from the stars, he thought of a name for the falls. He named them the Victoria Falls, after Queen Victoria of England.

As much as David would have liked to have stayed and watched the falls some more, he needed to keep moving. This time he decided to take a northeasterly route overland, cutting out a loop of the Zambezi River that wound south and then east before turning to the northeast again. Much to his surprise, David soon found himself on a high plateau, where the soil was fertile and moist but not waterlogged and there was an abundance of wild animals. He was certain the land would make good grazing land for cattle. Before long he had decided it would also be the perfect location for the northern missionary station he wanted to see established. He wrote a letter to the London Missionary Society detailing the land and asking it to send out missionaries as soon as possible before the opportunity to

establish a mission station there slipped away.
David was convinced he could find a practical route
to the coast from there, while a mission station on
the plateau could serve as the hub for a vast missionary enterprise in the area. Of course, he had no
way to send his letter, so he poked it away in a
leather pouch until he encountered civilization
again and could mail it.

After David became sick again, the expedition's
progress slowed. There were days when they
couldn't travel at all because David was too ill. And
then there were the many enemy villages they
passed through. David had to be constantly alert to
evil schemes and double-crossing chiefs. Regrettably, he lost two of his men within days of each
other. One died of fever and the other from a lion
attack.

As they approached Tetè, a Portuguese colony,
David became so ill that he sent some of his guides
on ahead of him. When the Portuguese army major
in Tete heard of David's plight, he immediately sent
a contingent of soldiers out to get him. The soldiers
escorted David into town with all the fanfare of roy-
alty. However, David was too ill to appreciate any
of it.

Days later, when he was beginning to feel a little
stronger, David had dinner with the major. The two
men discussed David's travels thus far. David was
particularly interested in finding out anything the
major might know about the stretch of river he had
bypassed after leaving Victoria Falls. The major
assured him the river was navigable all the way to

the falls, with just a few minor rapids to negotiate. Whether the major had ever seen these "minor" rapids or not, David never found out, but his casual comment was to result in much frustration for David Livingstone on his next trip.

Eventually, David felt strong enough to continue on. Since he knew he could travel the rest of the way by canoe down the river, when most of his Makalolo helpers asked if they could remain in Tete, David agreed. Sixteen Makalolos and five Portuguese soldiers paddled on down the Zambezi River with David. When they neared their destination, most of the remaining Makalolos asked if they could go back to Tete, and David let them. One man, Sekwebu, begged to stay with David. He said he wanted to see the Indian Ocean. While David felt the Makalolos should stay together, in the end he allowed Sekwebu to continue on with him.

In May 1856, David Livingstone, Sekwebu, and the five Portuguese soldiers arrived at the town of Quilimane in the delta of the Zambezi River. David had mapped the Zambezi all the way from its beginning at Lake Ngami to its end at the Indian Ocean. Now he was sure that missionaries and Christian traders could penetrate deep inland, opening up areas that had only been exploited by Arab slave traders until then.

In Quilimane, David was welcomed into the home of Colonel Nunes. The colonel had been expecting David and had some good news and some bad news for him. The good news was that a bundle of letters was waiting for him. The bad news was that five crewmen from the British ship *Dart* had drowned while negotiating the sandbars at the mouth of the river. The crewmen were returning to the ship after making a special trip to deliver David's mail. David was too sad to read the letters right away, but eventually he did open them. It seemed hollow praise when Roderick Murchison of the Royal Geographical Society wrote that David's first trip to the Atlantic Ocean had been "the greatest triumph in geographical research in our times."

David also received a letter from a publisher in London named John Murray, who said he was interested in publishing a book about David's travels in Africa. There were no letters, though, from Mary or his family, which caused David to begin to wonder whether he ought to go home to Scotland and see how everyone was. Once he added up his time spent traveling, he was astounded to find it had been nearly four and a half years since he had seen his family off in Port Elizabeth!

David secured passage on the HMS *Frolic* to the island of Mauritius in the Indian Ocean, where he would catch a steamer headed north into the Red Sea. When it came time for him to leave, Sekwebu once again begged to go with him. David was not enthusiastic, but in the end he gave in, and the two men climbed into a longboat for the perilous ride over the sandbar to where the ship was anchored.

The men made it to the HMS *Frolic* in one piece, but it was a rough trip to Mauritius. About halfway there, Sekwebu began acting very strangely. The captain warned David that Sekwebu was going mad from being on the ocean so long and suggested he should be shackled for his own safety. Although David could see that something was seriously wrong with Sekwebu, he could not bear to see his friend shackled like a slave. Regrettably, that night Sekwebu jumped overboard and drowned in the Indian Ocean, the ocean he had longed to see. David was very depressed about Sekwebu's death and chided himself for not taking the captain's advice.

In Mauritius David transferred to a steamer headed for Egypt via the Red Sea. As he crossed Egypt on his way to the Mediterranean Sea to catch still another steamer that would take him the rest of the way to Scotland, David intercepted a letter addressed to him. This letter was from his mother. David hoped it would cheer him up after Sekwebu's death, but the letter contained more bad news: David's father had died. David was devastated. He tormented himself with questions. Should he have gone home earlier? Were Mary and the children all right? Would he make it home before something else bad happened?

When the steamer he was traveling on had to dock in Marseilles, France, for emergency repairs, David became obsessed with getting home as soon as possible. He could not wait for the ship to be repaired, and he caught a train across France and a ship across the English Channel.

David had sent a message on ahead, and when he arrived in Southampton from France, Mary and the children were waiting for him. Waves of relief swept over David as he hugged his wife and children. They all looked fine and healthy, although five-year-old Zouga hung back and would not look his father in the eye. David couldn't blame him. He knew he was a stranger to his children.

David discovered to his dismay that Mary had not adjusted to staying in Scotland. She couldn't seem to get along with David's family, and in the end, she had left the children there and returned to London to stay with friends of her parents. She hadn't talked to David's family in over six months! David was devastated. All the time he had been trudging through the jungles and deserts of Africa he had imagined his family happy and comfortable back in Scotland. Now it seemed the family had been anything but.

David Livingstone was very much in demand in London. Within days of arriving in England, he was invited to a meeting of the Royal Geographical Society where he was honored with a gold medal. It was a complete surprise to David, who did not know what to say when he was asked to respond. After living so long among the Africans and speaking their dialects, he was not used to speaking English. Still, he had to say something. He cleared his throat. As he looked out on the assembled crowd, he spotted Cotton Oswell and Thomas Steele, his two old friends, and their presence gave him the courage to speak. "I am only doing my duty as a missionary in opening up a part of Africa to the sympathy of Christ," David said, looking squarely at the audience. "I am only just now buckling my armor for the good fight. I have no right to boast of anything. I will not boast until the last slave in Africa is free and Africa is open to honest trade and the light of Christianity." With that he bowed and left the podium.

An uproar of applause exploded, and everyone in the room rose to his feet. After the meeting, many people congratulated David, including John Murray, who was more eager than ever to have David Livingstone write a book.

David spent a great deal of time speaking in churches throughout England and Scotland on behalf of the London Missionary Society, urging more people to become missionaries to Africa. At the same time, the LMS was urging David to return to Africa and open a mission station of his own. It admired David's explorations and attempts to find trade and travel routes, but it did not share his enthusiasm that they would help spread the gospel message. Missionaries needed mission stations to be effective, it told him. All this made David think hard. His heart was really in trying to open up the Zambezi River area to trade and the gospel message.

It was then that David Livingstone received two amazing offers. One was an official government position in Africa that came with the title of "Her Majesty's Consul at Quilimane for the Eastern Coast and Independent Districts of the Interior." Along with the position came a salary of five hundred pounds a year, five times his missionary salary. The second offer was a publishing agreement to write a book to be called *Missionary Travels and Researches in South Africa*.

After thinking things over, David resigned from the London Missionary Society and accepted both offers. He felt it would be the most useful to the spread of Christianity in Africa to open up the Zambezi River as a highway for trade and the spread of the gospel message. Before returning to Africa to take up his new position, though, he settled in the London suburb of Chelsea with his family where he set to work writing his book.

The book took six months to complete. It contained 687 pages of maps, stories, journal entries, and observations, and it was an instant bestseller. The first printing of twelve thousand copies was ordered in advance and sold before a single book ever made it to a store. The book went straight into a second printing. Charles Dickens penned one of hundreds of reviews of the book. He wrote: "A narrative of great dangers and trials, encountered in a good cause by as honest and courageous a man as ever lived."

Privately David told Mary he would sooner cross Africa again than write another book! However, the income the book generated gave the Livingstones more money than they had ever had before, and David knew just what to do with it. He would pay for his three oldest children to stay with his mother and sisters in Scotland, where they could attend the best schools. He and Mary, along with Zouga, who was not yet in school, would return to Africa to take up his new position as Queen Victoria's representative and explore the Zambezi River.

Much to his surprise, Queen Victoria asked for a private audience with David. They chatted together for half an hour about his travels. When it was time to leave, David told Queen Victoria he was glad to have met her. Wherever he went in Africa the natives were shocked that he had never met his "big chief." This amused the queen, who inquired as to what else they asked. "Well," said David, "they ask me if you are very rich, and when I say yes, they press me to tell them how many cows you own!" Queen Victoria burst into hearty laughter, and David left Buckingham Palace feeling he had made a new friend.

On March 10, 1858, David and Mary Livingstone and their youngest son left to return to Africa aboard the *Pearl*. Between the pages of his Bible, David had tucked a poem Mary had given him the first night he arrived back in England fifteen months before. The last verse read:

You'll never part me, darling,
There's a promise in your eye,
I may tend you while I'm living, you will
*   watch me when I die,*
And if death but kindly lead me to the blessed
*   home on high,*
What a hundred thousand welcomes will
*   await you in the sky!"*

They left England with high hopes, but the verse of Mary's poem was to one day become a sad reality for them.

Chapter 16

Along the Zambezi River

The Livingstones were not the only passengers on the *Pearl*. Six other men were aboard whom the Royal Geographical Society had hired to help David explore the Zambezi River: Commander Bedingfeld of the Royal Navy; Dr. Kirk, a botanist and medical doctor; Richard Thornton, a geologist; Tom Baines, an artist; George Rae, an engineer; and David's younger brother Charles, who had been hired to be the "spiritual advisor" of the group.

David and the six men spent many hours huddled together planning their trip upriver as the Pearl tossed its way towards Cape Town. Although they made big plans, they had little idea of the hardships that lay ahead.

Stowed in three sections in the hold of the *Pearl* was a small, flat-bottomed paddlesteamer supplied by the British government. The men would bolt the three sections of the boat together when they reached their destination. The vessel had been named the *Ma-Robert* after Mary Livingstone. (The Africans called her Ma-Robert, or the mother of Robert, her oldest son.)

With favorable winds at her back, the *Pearl* made speedy progress and anchored off Cape Town in late April 1858. Robert Moffat was waiting to greet everyone and escort Mary and Zouga back to Kuruman. Mary and Zouga would wait at Kuruman until David had established a small base on the upper Zambezi River. Mary would then travel overland to join him. David refused to allow Mary or Zouga to go on with him right then because the lower Zambezi was too unhealthy for them to survive in. Besides, Mary was expecting another baby, and David did not want to risk another long trip with a child and a pregnant wife.

The *Pearl* sailed on from Cape Town to Quilimane. As soon as the men arrived there, David was glad that his wife was safely in Kuruman. Everything that could go wrong seemed to go wrong. Although the sections of the *Ma-Robert* were unloaded and quickly bolted together by George Rae, the boat's new design turned out to be defective. The vessel leaked constantly and needed enormous quantities of wood to stoke its boiler. Sometimes it took a day and a half to cut enough wood to keep the *Ma-Robert* running for a single day. It also took four hours for the boiler to build up enough steam to get the boat moving. And when the boat was finally running at full throttle, a child could paddle a canoe faster than the *Ma-Robert* moved. The draft of the boat, too, was deeper than expected, and the men often had to climb into the water, wade to the riverbank, and, using a rope, pull the boat off a sandbank it had run aground on.

All this would have been trying in the best of circumstances, but the state of the men's health turned the whole adventure into a nightmare. The men had all read David's book before leaving England, but they had failed to grasp just how uncomplaining David was about sickness and his own health. Malaria, which David had described in his book as "little worse than a common cold," gripped the men, along with its debilitating effects of giddiness, delirium, and constant vomiting. The men also suffered from mosquito bites, tropical ulcers, and ticks. They were not at all happy, and before long, arguments erupted among them. George Rae taunted Captain Bedingfeld by saying he knew how to run the boat better than the captain. Captain Bedingfeld, for his part, complained about everything. Charles Livingstone and Tom Baines were so ill with malaria they didn't leave their cabins for days at a time. And when they did, the others accused Charles of not doing any "real" work. David often found himself having to act like a parent trying to control squabbling children, and privately, even he thought they had a point about Charles!

It took the group three months to reach Tete, where David was glad to be reunited with the Makalolo helpers he had left there on his trip to the coast over two years before. Of the original one hundred men, seventy were still there. The other thirty men had either died of smallpox or been murdered. Still, those who remained had been treated well and were in no great hurry to return home to Linyanti. A few, though, did sign on as crew aboard the *Ma-Robert*. They had trusted David with their lives before, and he had not failed them.

As the *Ma-Robert* steamed slowly up the Zambezi River, it wheezed and labored so much that the crew nicknamed it the *Asthmatic*. After two of days travel upriver from Tete, the water became more turbulent, and huge round boulders began protruding from the river. David knew they were entering the Kebrabasa Gorge. On his trip to the coast two years earlier, however, the Portuguese army major in Tete had told him that the river was navigable all the way to the Victoria Falls and that there were just a few minor rapids along the way. David supposed that this was one of those minor rapids, and he expected to find a way through them. But as the water boiled and foamed over and around the boulders and the *Ma-Robert* fought to make headway against the surging current, David had to face reality. The boat could go no farther. But

David had come too far to give up. There had to be a way through the rapids. David decided he needed to do some exploring on foot to see how long the rapids were and find the best way through them.

"Come on," yelled David above the roar of the water. "I'm going ahead on foot."

Four Makalolo men stepped forward. "We are going with you," they announced.

"Me too," chimed in Dr. Kirk.

"All right," agreed David. "But you'll have to keep up with me or you'll be left behind."

The six men scrambled ashore and began climbing over the gigantic boulders. But the boulders were very smooth, and it was hard to get a good grip on them and not slip and slide. And the boulders were hot, blistering hot. None of this seemed to bother David, but the feet of the Makalolo men soon blistered, and the leather on the bottom of Dr. Kirk's boots was worn through, making it difficult going for him. Eventually, three of the Makalolos turned back, but David kept going. He was determined to find something that would give him hope. Eventually, he came to a three-hundred-foot high wall of rock covered with lichen. David, Dr. Kirk, and the remaining Makalolo man scaled the rock face together. When they reached the top, they got a panoramic and depressing view of what lay ahead. The rapids stretched on into the distance.

"There must be thirty miles of them!" exclaimed David, staring glumly down at the boulders and turbulent water of the river. "These are no minor rapids. There's no way we can ever get a boat through them."

No one spoke on the way back to the boat. David couldn't escape the reality of the situation. The Zambezi River was not navigable all the way to the Victoria Falls. There was going to be no easy river access to the plateau area where he'd imagined a great mission station being established. David was going to have to look elsewhere for a site for such a station. Reluctantly, he ordered the crew to turn the *Ma-Robert* around and head back to Tete.

Everyone on board the boat was tired of it by the time the boat got back to Tete. David immediately wrote to Roderick Murchison of the Royal Geographical Society asking if there was some way he could have a more powerful boat made and sent to Africa.

Next David decided to investigate the Shire River to the north and see if it led inland to some other promising areas. This time he left behind all the original crew except Dr. Kirk. The others were either too ill or too full of complaints to be worth the trouble of taking along.

The Shire River was filled with duckweed, which caught in the paddles of the *Ma-Robert* and became entwined in the engine, making constant stops necessary. As a result, progress up the river was laborious, but eventually the men came to a village called Magomero, which belonged to the Manganjis tribe. The climate in the area was reasonable, and the village was situated amid hills and away from the malaria swamps. David thought it would be a wonderful location for future missionary work. He called the area the Shire Highlands. As he traveled north from the village, David again encountered insurmountable rapids. This time there was also a waterfall, which he named after Roderick Murchison of the Royal Geographical Society, no doubt hoping it would help his request to the society for a bigger and better boat.

The men were forced to turn back, but two subsequent exploration trips up various arms of the Shire River proved more fruitful. In September 1859, David and Dr. Kirk found two lakes nestled between high mountains. The first, Lake Shirwa, was about fifty miles long, while the second, Lake Nyassa, was too large to map.

When the men got back to Tete after discovering the two lakes, several letters were waiting for David. One was from Mary. David was sure she had written to him before this, but somehow none of her other letters had made it through. His hands trembled as he opened the letter. As he read, two words jumped out at him: Anna Mary. Mary had had another baby on November 16, 1858, a whole year before! Mary wanted to know how soon she could come and join her husband and whether he had finished establishing a mission station on the upper Zambezi River. It was not easy for David to write back to her with the news that they had encountered mile upon mile of impassable rapids on the Zambezi River and that he had no idea when it would be safe for her to come and join him.

David also received a letter from the London Missionary Society informing him they were about to send out missionaries to work among the Makalolos. David groaned as he read. The Makalolos weren't ready for permanent missionaries. David hadn't yet had a chance to go back to Makalolo territory and see how things were and to talk with Chief Sekeletu about having permanent missionaries come and live among his people. But there was nothing David could do about it. By now the missionaries would be on their way to brave central Africa. Although David tried to have faith, he hated to think of what could happen to them.

In March 1860, a number of the Makalolo helpers who had traveled with David from Linyanti asked him to lead them home. They went by canoe as far as the Kebrabasa Gorge and then continued overland on foot. All along the way, they came across signs of slave trading. They walked through burned villages and came across huge piles of human bones and starving people. It saddened David, but it also strengthened his resolve to open the area up to trading and other civilizing influences. The way things stood at present, the tribe with the most guns and other weapons could terrorize anyone they pleased, and there were no laws or government to stop them.

As David, accompanied by Dr. Kirk, marched into the village of Sesheke in Makalolo territory, he looked forward to seeing Chief Sekeletu. He was shocked, however, when he finally laid eyes on him. The chief's body was covered with weeping sores, which the chief scratched constantly. Both David and Dr. Kirk made the same diagnosis: a severe form of eczema, that had turned the chief into a cringing wreck. They treated him as best they could with zinc sulfate ointment, and the sores began to heal. David knew, though, that once the ointment ran out, the eczema would return.

Whether it was from being sick for so long, David could not tell, but Chief Sekeletu had changed a great deal since the two men had last been together. The chief had blamed many of his people for putting a sickness spell on him, and the witch doctor had performed many ritual killings. David could see that the Makalolo people did not have the love and respect for their chief that they formerly had.

Dr. Kirk went to investigate a rumor he had heard about some white people in nearby Linyanti. He returned with grim news. Two families, consisting of four adults and five children, had indeed been sent out by the London Missionary Society. Regrettably, Dr. Kirk had not been able to see the people in person because all that was left to see was some graves. Three adults and three children had all died within weeks of arriving in Linyanti. The last surviving adult and two children had fled overland in the direction of Kuruman. David felt ill. These people's deaths had been so pointless, and he chided himself that he may have unwittingly contributed to them by giving such stirring talks about the need for missionaries when he was back in England.

David did not want to stay long in Makalolo. On September 17, 1860, he and Dr. Kirk began the trip back to the coast. Along the way, David became convinced they could shoot the Kebrabasa Rapids in their canoes. He was partly right. His canoe managed to navigate around the thousands of boulders, but Dr. Kirk was not able to do the same. The canoe capsized, sending all of Dr. Kirk's books, journals, and medical instruments into the turbulent water. And while Dr. Kirk himself was rescued, everything he owned was lost.

By the time the men reached Tete, David was feeling gloomy. And on top of everything else, the *Ma-Robert* became stranded on a sandbar. By this time, David had had enough of the troublesome vessel, and he abandoned it and left it to rot where it had run aground!

In January 1862, David received a letter he both dreaded and wanted. Mary had given up waiting for the "right" time to join her husband. She was catching a ship from Cape Town to Quilimane and would be arriving at the end of the month. For the time being, she would leave Zouga and Anna with her parents in Kuruman. When she and David had established a permanent home, she would go back and collect them.

Traveling on the same ship with Mary were the wives of four missionaries David had already escorted to Magomero in the Shire Highlands where they were establishing a mission station. These missionaries were from the Universities Mission of

Central Africa, which was established after David had spoken at both Oxford and Cambridge universities while in England. The students had been so inspired by what David said that they banded together to send missionaries to Africa.

It was strange for David and Mary to see each other again. It had been four years since they had last been together, and David was now much gaunter. He assumed that Mary would travel up to the new mission station at Magomero with the other wives and stay there, but Mary had other ideas. She told David she would not be separated from him, no matter what he said. Realizing how stubborn his wife was, David gave in, though he hated to think of her living in the swampy areas that his responsibilities seemed to keep him in.

As it turned out, either choice would have been fatal. The missionary wives were to be met halfway to Magomero by their husbands and so set out with their guides. It had rained for days in the area, and the husbands were delayed. While they waited for the men to arrive, the wives succumbed to dysentery, malaria, and hunger. They were all dead by the time their husbands arrived to meet them.

Mary and David spent two and a half happy months together. David was busy assembling a small steamboat that had been sent out from England on the same ship that brought Mary and the missionary wives. The boat, which David had designed himself, was called the *Lady Nyassa*, after the lake he hoped to explore with her. David had paid six thousand pounds for the boat, most of the money coming from sales of his book, but as he worked on her, he knew it would be worth it. She was a sturdy vessel and well-suited to shallow river work.

In April 1862, Mary became ill with malaria. It was her first encounter with the disease, and her body did not respond well. With David and Dr. Kirk attending to her night and day, she had the best medical care in Africa, but it was not enough. Her health slipped away, and on April 27, within a week of falling ill, Mary died at the age of forty-one. David buried her under a huge baobab tree. As he stood at his wife's grave, he recalled the words from her poem, written with such tenderness and hope: *I may tend you while I'm living, you will watch me when I die.*

It had been true. Mary had come to be at his side, to help him and take care of his needs, and now he had watched her die. Africa had claimed the life of the one he loved the most, and for the first time since arriving on the continent, David wondered whether he had the will to go on. In his journal he wrote, "I wept over her who well deserved many tears. I loved her when I married her, and the longer I lived with her I loved her the more…. For the first time in my life I feel willing to die."

But it was not time for David Livingstone to give up. He still had important work to do.

Chapter 17

Still Headed Inland

India!" gasped George Rae. "You can't be serious, Livingstone. You're going to sail the *Lady Nyassa* to India? Whatever would make you want to go on such a suicide trip?"

David looked at his old friend. George Rae was the last man still with him from the group who'd come to Africa six years before to help explore the Zambezi River. "I need to go home," he said. "The two years since Mary died have not been easy. I need to see my children again. Little Anna Mary is five now, and I've never laid eyes on her. And now that I've explored six hundred miles up the Rovuma River, I need to go and report that it's too shallow for a steamboat to navigate."

"Yes, yes, I understand all that. And quite right, too. It's a good thing to regroup in Scotland, but what does that have to do with sailing the *Lady Nyassa* to India?" pressed George Rae.

David smiled wearily. "I've spent my life trying to find ways to stop the slave trade, and I will not leave my boat in Africa where it can fall into the hands of slave traders and be used to further their evil practice. Besides, I paid for it with money from my book, and I've been thinking I might sell it and use the money for the two youngest children's education. I'm sure I can find someone in India who would use it for a good purpose."

"But you'll never make it to India." blurted George Rae. "You can't be thinking straight. India is twenty-five hundred miles away, and there are monsoons in that part of the world. The *Lady Nyassa* is a riverboat, not an oceangoing vessel. She's only forty feet long from stem to stern and doesn't have sails—only a tiny steam engine. It's insane! She'll break apart at the first big wave, and you'll all be drowned."

"I take it you're not coming with me, then?" asked David dryly.

"I'd follow you to the ends of the earth, but not to the bottom of the ocean!" George Rae replied. "Be reasonable for once, David. This scheme of yours will not work."

However, the *Lady Nyassa* did set sail for India on April 30, 1864, with twelve crew members aboard, three white men and nine Africans. None of the men had any ocean sailing experience, and seven of the Africans came from inland villages and had never even seen the ocean before the voyage. Still, somehow David managed to keep his crew from jumping overboard and sail the *Lady Nyassa* up the east coast of Africa to Zanzibar. From there the boat sailed east to Bombay, India, arriving on June 13, 1864.

In Bombay, no one was expecting a small riverboat from Africa, and no welcoming committee was waiting. However, David was viewed as a hero throughout the British Empire, and once he was able to convince the port authorities that he really had sailed all the way from Africa, he was given an official welcome. He even had an audience with Sir Bartle Frere, the governor of Bombay. Sir Bartle Frere was captivated by David's efforts to end slave trading and offered to help in any way he could. However, he could not recommend a buyer for the *Lady Nyassa*, so David left the boat in the care of a British naval officer. He found a new home in Bombay for his African crew, and caught a ship bound for England.

David arrived in London on July 23, 1864, and much to his surprise he received a hero's welcome. His first night home he was swept off to a reception at Prime Minister Palmerston's home. For the rest of the week he kept busy with appointments to see the foreign secretary and other important government officials.

By the end of the week, David was anxious for all the formalities to be over so that he could visit his family. Once in Scotland, the reunion with his family was a mixture of joy and sadness. His eighty-year-old mother was now senile and didn't recognize him. His two sisters, Janet and Agnes, were overworked taking care of their mother and raising his children, especially since Zouga and Anna had been sent to Scotland from Kuruman. Much to David's dismay, his eighteen-year-old son Robert had gone off to Africa in search of him. When he couldn't locate David, he had drifted on to the United States, where he'd enlisted in the Union Army to fight in the Civil War. The whole family waited nervously for news from him. Meanwhile, fifteen-year-old Thomas was ill with kidney disease. David knew it was a serious condition and worried about his son's recovery. The other three children, seventeen-year-old Agnes, twelve-year-old Zouga, and five-year-old Anna, all seemed to be well, though Anna was very shy around the father she had not previously met.

While in Scotland, David began writing a second book, entitled the *Narrative of an Expedition to the Zambezi and Its Tributaries.* He also gave lectures on how Africa needed to be opened up to commerce and how the slave trade needed to be stopped.

Since his official duties exploring and mapping the Zambezi River area were now complete, the British government gave David five hundred pounds to return to Africa and look for ways to end the slave trade. The Royal Geographical Society also gave him five hundred pounds. As well, James

Young, David's old friend from his days at Anderson College, gave David another one thousand pounds. James Young had made a fortune inventing paraffin oil, which was used widely in lamps because it was so clean burning.

In August 1865, David Livingstone left England for the last time. As he left, his heart was heavy. His mother had died during his time at home, and just before boarding the ship, he received news that his oldest son Robert had died in a prisoner-of-war camp in North Carolina.

The ship took David back to Bombay so that he could sell the *Lady Nyassa* and collect his crew and take them back to Africa. In Bombay, Sir Bartle Frere took an active interest in David's work and raised one thousand pounds to help pay for David's next expedition. David also found a buyer for the *Lady Nyassa*, though he got only 2,300 pounds for it. This was much less than it was worth, but as it turned out, it did not matter. David put the money in a bank in Bombay, planning to send it to Scotland later to pay for Zouga and Anna's education. Within weeks of depositing the money, however, the banks in India failed, and David lost every penny he'd received for the boat.

Besides giving David the thousand pounds, Sir Bartle Frere offered David and his men a free trip to Zanzibar aboard the *Thule*, a steamship he was sending as a gift to the Sultan of Zanzibar. In Zanzibar, David was reunited with Dr. Kirk, who was now the British consul there.

From Zanzibar, David caught another ship down the coast to Mikindani at the mouth of the Rovuma River. In Mikindani, David hired a fresh group of men to go with him on his next expedition. Among them were Susi and Chuma, two ex-slaves whom David had freed. These two men proved to be faithful helpers, but David did not have the same experience with his choice of other helpers. Many of the men in his expedition deserted him, and on January 20, 1867, two men fled with David's most important possession, his medicine box. David knew it was only a matter of time before he came down with another bout of malaria or dysentery, which, without medicines, he knew could kill him. Still, stubborn as he was, he chose to keep going. What he did not know was that the two men were cunning enough to return to Mikindani and report David Livingstone's death so that they could receive their wages. They offered David's medicine box as proof of his death. No one knew for sure whether their story was true. Was the great explorer really dead, or was he still slogging on through the bush somewhere?

A search party was organized, and although it did not catch up with David, its members became convinced that he was still alive and still headed inland. And he was. On April 4, 1867, David arrived at the southern end of Lake Tanganyika. By then, the sicknesses he feared had caught up with him, and he had to rest for several weeks before going on. He decided to explore the western side of the lake.

The sights that awaited him there turned his stomach more than his sickness did. Everywhere there were signs of slave trade. Huts were burned, villages destroyed, and dead bodies strewn along the trails. At one point, David came upon a woman with her three-year-old son. The child, who was about to be sold into slavery, clung to his mother and wept bitterly. David watched in despair as the boy was handed over in return for four yards of fabric.

The slave traders in this area were Arabs, and while David despised what they were doing, he recognized that they needed to hear the gospel message. Because of this, he struck up many friendships with the slave traders, often traveling with them. He was always respectful towards them and took every opportunity possible to tell them about the gospel message and how God wanted them to stop their horrible trade. The slave traders in turn were kind to David, and without their help, David may well have died from recurring bouts of malaria.

For the next several years, David Livingstone explored the inland areas. Sometimes he traveled with only six helpers, and sometimes he traveled with large groups of Arabs. Wherever he went, he took notes and made maps of everything he saw. In the course of his travels, he discovered two more lakes, Bangwelo and Moreo. Then in 1870, he heard that he was very close to a river the Africans called Lualaba. It was said that the river was as wide as twenty canoes and very deep, and it flowed north.

David wondered whether this could be the upper reaches of the Nile. That would be quite a discovery. If it was the Nile, it would most likely be navigable all the way to Egypt and the Mediterranean Sea. The alternative was that the Lualaba was part of the Congo River system. If it was, it would be useless as a way to open up the interior of Africa. The Congo River, which flowed into the Atlantic Ocean, was not navigable seventy-five miles from its mouth because of a series of rapids that stretched inland for a hundred miles. Of course, there was only one way to discover whether the Lualaba was part of the Congo River or the Nile. David would have to canoe down it and see where it took him.

By January 1871, fifty-eight-year-old David Livingstone was camped on the banks of the Lualaba River near the village of Nyangwe. If he had not been so ill, he would not have spent a day there. It was the worst place he had visited in all of Africa. Not only had the slave traders created havoc in the area, but the people in the village were themselves enthusiastic cannibals. To show how important they were, the men all wore necklaces decorated with human jawbones. David could hardly wait to get well enough to be on his way, and by October, he had found a more hospitable village called Ujiji.

Although David was happy to be away from Nyangwe, his life was still filled with concerns. He was too far from the coast to hear news from home or get fresh supplies. By the end of October, he had run out of just about everything. His teeth were shattered and broken from eating the tough local corn. And when his India ink supply ran out, he was forced to crush seeds to make a watery red ink, which he used to write his notes on the edges of pieces of old newspapers.

David lived in limbo. He was not well enough to go forward with his exploration, and he was far too stubborn to go back. Then on the morning of November 3, 1871, David's faithful helper Susi came running into his hut.

"Master, master. I see an Englishman! He is like you! He is coming here," Susi said excitedly.

David pulled himself up from his cot. "Calm down, Susi, and tell me exactly what you saw."

Before Susi had time to explain, David saw for himself. Winding along the dusty trail was a large party of porters led by a single white man carrying an American flag. The group kept coming until it stopped in front of David.

The white man, who seemed to be about half David's age, looked David in the eye and asked, "Doctor Livingstone, I presume?"

David tipped his cap. "Yes," he replied. "And who might you be?'

"I am Henry Stanley, Doctor, and I have been sent to find you!"

David laughed. As far he was concerned, he'd never been lost. "Come and sit down," he said with a flourish, pointing to his tiny hut.

David Livingstone and Henry Stanley sat talking for a long time. Henry had with him the most precious cargo of all—letters from home. As David read them, he learned that his daughter Agnes had married, while son Thomas was alive, though still very sick, and his in-laws, Robert and Mary Moffatt, had returned to Scotland to live. There were newspapers, too, that told of huge breakthroughs. The Suez Canal had been opened, connecting the Red Sea with the Mediterranean. Now a person could sail from the east coast of Africa to England without having to travel overland through Egypt. And a railroad now joined the east and west coasts of the United States.

After David had read all his mail and the newspapers, Henry Stanley told him the purpose for his visit. He was a newspaper reporter for the *New York Herald*. David Livingstone had become a legend in America, and everyone wanted to know whether he was alive and what he was up to.

Despite being a reporter, Henry Stanley, like David, had a great sense of adventure. It was not long before the two men had decided to explore Lake Tanganyika together. Henry generously shared his provisions and food, the best David had eaten in months. Henry also bought a canoe for the exploration and a donkey for David to ride on. Even so, the pair made slow progress. It took them a month to discover that the water at the northern end ran *into* the lake and not out of it. It seemed very unlikely that the lake was the source of the Nile River, as David had hoped it would be.

David returned to Ujiji discouraged and ill once again. Henry Stanley stayed with him, nursed him, and helped him to put his journals into order. Over the next three months, Henry did everything he could think of to convince David Livingstone to return to the coast with him. He even offered to go with David to Scotland, where David could get good medical care and see his family. But as appealing as the offer was, David had set himself a goal. He would find a waterway into the interior of Africa, or he would die trying.

Finally, in May 1872, Henry Stanley said farewell to his new friend and headed back to the coast. With him he carried all of David's journals and a large number of letters David had written to friends and family. It would be the last time any white person would see David Livingstone alive.

It was five months after Henry Stanley had departed before David felt strong enough to take his next trip. This time he decided to go south until he reached the end of Lake Tanganyika. Then he would turn west down the Lualaba River and see where it led to.

As on David's previous trips, the African wilderness proved filled with unwelcome surprises. David's small party of men found themselves slogging through swamps of waist-deep thick, black mud. They were also attacked by bees, and menacing lions hungrily stalked their campsites each night.

On March 19, 1873, David celebrated his sixtieth birthday, though it was not a happy occasion. He was now in constant pain and unable to travel for more than ten hours a week. For someone who had traversed more than forty thousand miles of African wilderness, this was pitifully slow progress, and David found it difficult to accept. But he had no alternative but to accept it; his body was worn and tired.

David continued writing in his journal, though even this tired him to the point where most days it took all his effort to write a sentence. During this time he made the following entries:

21 April—tried to ride, but was forced to
   lie down and they carried me back to
   the village exhausted.
22 April—carried in kitanda *[stretcher]*
   S.W. 2 1/2 *[hours of travel]*.
23 April—ditto. 1 1/2 *[hours]*.
24 April—ditto 1.
25 April—ditto 1.
26 April—ditto. 2 1/2 to Kalunganjofu's.

Total for week = 8 1/2 *[hours of travel]*.

On April 27, David was too weak to write anything in his journal. He was camped on the shore of Lake Bangwelo, and it was raining heavily. His African helpers quickly built him a hut to keep the rain out. The next morning, the chief of the area, Chitambo, came to visit David. For the first time in his life, David Livingstone was too weak to talk to a chief.

By April 30, 1873, it was clear to David that he was very seriously ill. He asked Susi to give him some medicine, and then he fell into a fitful sleep.

Sometime during the next two hours, David climbed from his cot and got down on his knees. He rested his elbows on the edge of the bed and put his hands together to pray. He was still in that position when Susi and Chuma found him dead several hours later.

Chapter 18

Servant of Humanity

David Livingstone's three African helpers, Susi, Chuma, and Jacob Wainwright, were faced with a problem. Their friend was dead, and they didn't know what to do with his body. In the years they had been with David, they had come to understand he was considered a great man in his homeland, and they wondered if it was right to bury him in a tiny village on the shore of a lake deep in the heart of Africa. David would probably not have cared, but his three loyal helpers decided that somehow they would get his body back to Great Britain. It was no small task, but they promised one another they would do whatever was necessary to make it happen.

The first thing the three men did was cut David's body open and remove all his internal organs, including his heart, which they buried under a mvula tree. Next they covered his body with salt and left it to dry in the sun for two weeks. They guarded his body day and night to make sure no wild animals tried to eat it. Once the body was dry, they wrapped it in tree bark and then sewed it inside a sheath of sailcloth. They lashed the sheath to a long pole and sealed it all with tar. Now the body was airtight and ready to be carried to the coast.

Although the journey was over one thousand miles, never once did the three Africans consider abandoning David Livingstone's body. They carried it through war zones, swamps, and jungles. They even met an expedition of white men headed inland who tried to convince them it was too dangerous to continue on and they should bury David's body where they were. But they would not. As they told one African who asked, "This is a very, very big man!"

Africans had many superstitions about carrying dead bodies, and at one stage, the men were attacked and harassed. After that, they rewrapped David's body and told everyone it was a large bolt of cloth they were taking to market!

When they reached the coast eight months later, they delivered the body to the British authorities, who transported it to England aboard the HMS *Vulture*. Since Jacob Wainwright spoke better English than Susi and Chuma and could also read and write the language, he was chosen to accompany David's body on its final journey. Once he reached London, an autopsy was carried out to ensure that it was in fact the body of Doctor David Livingstone. The broken bones in his upper left arm from his encounter with the lion were ample proof of his identity.

Now that everyone was assured it was the body of David Livingstone, April 18, 1874, was declared a day of national mourning throughout the British Isles. There was not a student or factory worker anywhere in the country who did not know that Britain's greatest hero was being buried that day. Eleven and a half months after he had died, David Livingstone was finally laid to rest during a huge funeral service at Westminster Abbey. Mourners overflowed from the church into the streets outside.

Eight pallbearers carried the coffin. Among them were Thomas Steele, now Sir Thomas Steele, and Cotton Oswell, two friends from David's early expeditions; Dr. Kirk, who had helped David explore the Zambezi River; Henry Stanley, the last white man to see David alive; and Jacob Wainwright, who had helped transport David's body from the interior back to England. Robert Moffat, David's father-in-law, sat in the front row, along with the Livingstone children.

A huge slab of black marble was placed on David Livingstone's grave. On it were inscribed some words taken from a letter David had written to a friend a year before he died. David had been writing about his most passionate subject, ending slavery. The words read: "All I can say in my solitude is may Heaven's rich blessings come down on every-one—American, English, Turk—who will help to heal this open sore of the world."

A month after the funeral, the United Free Church of Scotland decided to establish a mission station in Central Africa in honor of David's work there. The mission was to be built on the edge of Lake Nyassa, and it would be called Livingstonia. Ten thousand pounds was quickly raised from Scottish churches, and Livingstonia soon consisted of a mission, a school, an industrial settlement, and a hospital.

In 1913, the Royal Geographical Society held a special meeting to commemorate David Living-stone's birth in Scotland one hundred years earlier. Lord Cruzon, president of the society, summed up David Livingstone's life perhaps better than anyone else: "In the course of his wonderful career, Livingstone served three masters. As a missionary he was the sincere and zealous servant of God. As an explorer he was the indefatigable servant of science. As a denouncer of the slave trade he was the fiery servant of humanity."

Arnold, Richard. *The True Story of David Livingstone, Explorer.* Children's Press, 1957.

Blaike, W. Garden. *The Personal Life of David Livingstone.* Fleming H. Revell, 1880.

Listowel, Judith. *The Other Livingstone.* Charles Scribner's Sons, 1974.

Livingstone, David. *Family Letters, Volumes One & Two.* edited by I. Schapera. Chatto & Windus, 1959.

Simmons, Jack. *Livingstone and Africa.* English Universities Press, 1955.

Wellman, Sam. *David Livingstone, Missionary and Explorer.* Barbour Publishing, Inc., 1995.

Janet and Geoff Benge are a husband and wife writing team with over fifteen years of writing experience. Janet is a former elementary school teacher. Geoff holds a degree in history. Originally from New Zealand, the Benges spent ten years serving with Youth With A Mission. They have two daughters, Laura and Shannon, and an adopted son, Lito. They make their home in the Orlando, Florida, area.